Praise for *Blessing My Demons*

"If you've ever been besieged by your inner critic while striving to achieve your dreams, Chelsea Forbrook's guide to taming and transforming these demons will not only prove an invaluable guide in how to overcome them, it will also make you laugh—and demons *hate* being laughed at! Seriously, just about everybody trying to do anything new or good in the world has got this problem—so *everyone* needs to read this book!"

—**Sean W. Murphy**, NEA creative writing fellow, Hemingway Award-winning novelist, and Zen meditation teacher (murphyzen.com)

"With breathtaking honesty, Chelsea Forbrook not only reveals, but literally illustrates, her various inner critics in all their petty, outrageous, and often hilarious glory. In doing so, she invites readers to be just as honest about what is actually going on inside their own psyche.

It can be challenging and even confronting to take an honest look at ourselves in this way, but Chelsea's sincerity, warmth, and compassion permeate every page and helped me keep going. Her engaging voice and compelling personal stories made me feel that I had a companion—a soul friend—on the journey of facing and blessing my demons."

—**Jenny Campbell**, Riso-Hudson certified Enneagram teacher (enneawake.com)

"*Blessing My Demons* is at once poignant and powerful. For anyone who has ever battled with their inner critic (who hasn't?!), this is the book for you. Chelsea Forbrook tells the intimate story of her journey with humor, curiosity, and compassion. You will resonate with many of the demon characters, and you will laugh, cry, and lament alongside. That alone is the crucial first step towards taming and healing, understanding, and freedom."

—**Yenkuei Chuang**, Ph.D., writer, clinical psychologist, and mindfulness teacher (yenkuei.org)

"*Blessing My Demons* is engaging, insightful, and soul-baring. Chelsea Forbrook digs down to the essentials of what it means to be a human and comes out laughing and hopeful and inviting the rest of us to join the fun. The depth of vulnerability in this book is enough to make me shake in my boots, while inspiring me to open myself to the transformation of my own heart."

—**Rev. Phil Gebben Green**, Presbyterian pastor and Enneagram Prison Project faculty (enneagramprisonproject.org)

"In the Enneagram world, conversations about 'the inner critic' often get stuck in descriptions of Type 1s, as if they are the only people to struggle with those pesky lying voices. In this boldly vulnerable book, Chelsea Forbrook tenderly invites us all to notice the lies we tell ourselves. Then—with personal stories, light-hearted illustrations, and practical exercises—she helps readers compassionately whisper to our inner demons so they shut the f*** up. I am confident I will recommend this book to clients for years to come."

—**Stephanie J. Spencer**, Enneagram coach and author of *Out of the Box & Into the Wild: An Enneagram Journey through the Triads of Nature* (www.stephaniejspencer.com)

"Taking a compassionate and clear-eyed look at our inner critic is a necessary exercise to heal and thrive—for ourselves, our relationships, our communities, and our world. Chelsea Forbrook vividly and viscerally brings fresh insight to how to work with the harsh, sneaky inner critic from a place of awareness and acceptance. Each chapter ends with spot-on inner work exercises, and I fell in love with the liberating love letters that bless and release the named and tamed demons.

This is a sometimes irreverent, humorous, holy, and vital exploration on how to unlock our feelings, live more grounded in life as it is, and learn how to love the process of awakening. It will break you open and enrich your life today and all along the way."

—**Kathy Jankowski**, consultant and guide to conscious living and working, certified Robert Peng Qigong trainer, certified Level 3 breath coach, and Enneagram instructor (kathyjankowski.com)

"*Blessing My Demons* will motivate you to let go of your inner critics and open yourself to more self-love and freedom. This book contains transformational tools you will use again and again to let go of your inner critics. It is honest, grounding, transformative, fun, and motivational. Chelsea Forbook has infused this book with the sweet energy of self-love. You will feel it radiate into your heart from every page. *Blessing My Demons* inspired me to quiet my critical voices and listen to my heart's voice of self-love. If you wish to totally love yourself, this gem is a must-read!"

—**Anne Mureé**, Enneagram master coach and founder and president of Olive Branchways, a consulting firm which uses the Enneagram in transformational coaching and education (annemuree.com)

Blessing My Demons

How to Name, Tame, and Transform Your Inner Critic

CHELSEA FORBROOK

*To protect the privacy of certain individuals, some names
and identifying details have been changed.*

Blessing My Demons © copyright 2023 by Chelsea Forbrook. All rights reserved. No part of this book may be reproduced in any form whatsoever, by photography or xerography or by any other means, by broadcast or transmission, by translation into any kind of language, nor by recording electronically or otherwise, without permission in writing from the author, except by a reviewer, who may quote brief passages in critical articles or reviews.

ISBN 13: 978-1-63489-662-7

Library of Congress Catalog Number has been applied for.
Printed in the United States of America
First Printing: 2023
27 26 25 24 23   5 4 3 2 1

Cover & interior design by Kimberly Glyder

Wise Ink
PO Box 580195
Minneapolis, MN 55458-0195

Wise Ink is a creative publishing agency for game-changers. Wise Ink authors uplift, inspire, and inform, and their titles support building a better and more equitable world. For more information, visit wiseink.com

To order, visit itascabooks.com or www.chelseaforbrook.com.
Reseller discounts available.

*This book is dedicated to you, dear reader,
that you may awaken to the Love within and all around;
that you might lean into your evolutionary impulse
to adapt, heal, and thrive.*

Table of Contents

Acknowledgments	1

Part 1: Name It

An Important Overview	7
What Is an Inner Critic?	11

Part 2: Tame It

My Two Masters, Vader and Yoda	33
Missy Prissy	47
Sister Mary Chastity Constance of the Immaculate Righteousness	63
The Imposter Police	79
The Locker Room Boys	95
Satan and the Street Preacher	111
Granny Divine	129
The Boss of Bludgeon	139
Thoressa	153

Part 3: Transform It

What Do Emotions Have to Do with This?	171
Spiritual Friendship	183
Emergence of the Inner Advocate	197
The End of an Era	205
Detaching from the Inner Critic	223

Final Blessing   237

Acknowledgments

There are so many people I would like to thank for helping me through the process of writing my first book. This book would never have expanded past a fleeting idea in my mind were it not for Sean Murphy and Tania Casselle's mentorship and structured guidance through their year-long writing class, Write to the Finish. Thank you to Yenkuei for our accountability check-ins and your encouragement. Your deep presence kept me motivated to stay the course.

Thank you to Janet for holding space for me for over a decade in spiritual direction, helping me heal the wounds inflicted by my Inner Critic and learn to trust my gut and my heart's deepest desires.

Thank you to my Enneagram teachers—Anne Mureé, Michael Naylor, Russ Hudson, and Jenny Campbell—for reminding me again and again that my ego, my perfectionism, and my Inner Critic don't define me; for teaching me about the Essence of who I actually am, which is goodness and sacredness—qualities that are always available to me through stillness and Presence.

Thank you to Mark Nunberg and the Common Ground Meditation Center community, for teaching me that compassion for myself and others is always an option and for showing me how to actually practice it, moment to moment, whether on the cushion or off.

Thank you to the Minneapolis Twelve Step community, for listening to my shame, anger, and fear with nothing but acceptance and love. You taught me that I am *worth* doing all this inner work and healing. You told me I deserved to be happy, joyous, and free; and you believed this for me until I could believe it for myself.

Thank you to my parents, for introducing me to prayer, Jesus, and scripture. Despite the "heretical and heathen" ways I've chosen in adulthood, this early education is a foundation I will carry with me and cherish always.

A big shout-out to my friends, who in many ways have become family. We have grown together, laughed together, failed together, and shared countless resources, both internal and external. You have cheered me on through thick and thin. It's cheesy but true: You *are* the wind beneath my wings.

And most importantly, to all the Spiritual Ancestors around the globe. You have carried the torch of sacred tradition throughout the ages, passing the Gospel, the Dharma, the spiritual practices, the psychological maps, the songs, the rituals, and the sacred stories from generation to generation, audaciously believing that your mission mattered in this epic adventure called the Evolution of Humankind. Your work has not been in vain. My life is forever changed because of you, and it is with deep Gratitude and Humility that I now attempt to pass on a fraction of the Wisdom you have given me.

May this book, and my life, be an instrument of the Mysterious Love that animates the whole Universe.

PART 1

Name It

CHAPTER 1:
An Important Overview

    I believe, despite the distracting chaos and pain of the world right now, that we are in a collective process of waking up and maturing our souls. Everywhere I go, I find that people are interested in doing transformational inner work because they have a deep sense that there is more to life than what we've historically been told. The old narratives no longer serve us. We no longer agree to settle for the attitude of "just survive and work hard until you die." We're not being fooled anymore. We know that things like marriage, kids, or working our way up the promotional ladder won't bring us lasting satisfaction in and of themselves. We feel the call to something more. It is the call to Wake Up.

    In Western culture, humans have such a deficit of self-esteem, true confidence, and self-love. We seem desperate to find it, and many are looking for it in places that only make things worse. But people *are* searching, as they have done for ages—and that is a good thing.

    This book is a guide to self-awareness and healing, on both spiritual and psychological levels. It does not contain a secret formula to happiness (spoiler alert!), but it *is* a compass helping to point the way Home. Unfortunately, there is no one-size-fits-all, fast-track equation for enlightenment. Awakening is an organic unfolding, uniquely personal to each individual.

How to Read This Book

    In this book, I share pieces of my journey that I hope will shed some light on your path. At the very least, hopefully it can give you a good laugh. I have included a broad range of spiritual practices and exercises at the end of each chapter. They are not there simply to be read through. They are meant to be *done*. Try them out. Stop, reflect, and *do* the practices before reading on.

Some people will want to zip through this book, then go back and do the exercises. That works too. Just do them. Not all of them will be a good fit for you, but you won't know until you try. It is my hope that you take some of these practices with you into your daily life and stick with them over time. That is what will make the difference between this being an "interesting" book or a "life-changing" book. But that difference is up to you, dear reader.

It will be helpful for you to designate a specific notebook, journal, or sketchbook as your Inner Critic Journal. The exercises build on each other, so it will be good to have them all in one place so that you can easily reference earlier exercises you have completed. One of the main practices I work with (and I encourage you to do the same) is drawing my Inner Critic voices as characters. If you don't consider yourself an artist, don't panic! Stick figures will do just fine. The point is to get the voices out of your head and on to paper. As long as these Inner Voices remain subconscious, they have power. Our work throughout this book will be to make the subconscious conscious.

As I was writing this book, I had several Inner Critic attacks myself, such as, *Why would anyone want to read my rambling thoughts when there are already other great books out there on this topic?* With some soul-searching and clear thinking, I realized I do have a unique voice on this subject—*and* I wanted to create a book on the Inner Critic that was lighthearted and humorous. If this work doesn't contain some fun, it's just too much to bear. Learning to laugh at ourselves and be playful is part of the healing journey. As you will soon discover, I am quite irreverent. (Forgive me, Jesus, for the many heretical jokes I make about you! Actually, I know you don't give a shit.)

Throughout this book, I will be using references to Christian, Buddhist, and Twelve Step recovery teachings that are universal to the human path toward wholeness. You needn't identify with any of these traditions to find assistance and deep meaning from their instruction. I use these teachings because these are the ones I am most familiar with, the roads which I have traversed. I was raised Christian and began sincerely incorporating Buddhist and Twelve

AN IMPORTANT OVERVIEW

Step teachings in my late twenties. I have a deep respect for their wisdom and power due to the ways they have "saved me" from myself. If you ascribe to other traditions (or to no tradition at all), have no fear! This book will still be relevant to you, since the commonality of our lived human *experience* is quite surprising.

Throughout this book, there are various references to God, Higher Power, the Source, etc. Don't let the term *God* trip you up if you're not into theism. It is just pointing to something benevolent that is greater than our ego. You can translate to whatever word you like best. "The Universe" works for many people. The Buddha, Dhamma, and Sangha are collectively a tried-and-true refuge. Mother Nature, Spirit, the Intelligent Energy that animates all life, Consciousness Itself, Inner Wisdom, our True Essence, or Big Mind are all equally appropriate replacements too. After all, they are all pointing to a Great Mystery that cannot be named: the "I Am that I Am," found deep within and everywhere without.

While it's a bit goofy, I have changed my spelling of *God* to *Godde* in many places. I did not make this up. This idea comes from a Biblical translation called *The Divine Feminine Version of the New Testament*.[1] There are a few reasons its translators chose this term and why I adopted it for myself. One is that so many people have accumulated emotional baggage—and even trauma—around the word *God*. For many, it is a word that can trigger images of damnation, judgment, exclusion, and fear. That's not what we're going for! Let's get as far away from that as possible!

The second reason for this spelling is that it is a visual reminder that the Ultimate Source of Love embodies masculine *and* feminine qualities. Why would we ever trust a Divine Energy that is void of nurture, compassion, kindness, and tender care? That would be foolishness! With the long-awaited worldwide awakening of the Divine Feminine within all traditions across the world, we are in need of a gender-inclusive word for the Source. *Godde* is halfway between *God* and *goddess*. Since many of us are programmed to envision a grumpy old white man in the sky when we hear or read the word *God*, this new spelling helps rewire the brain and opens us up to endless possibilities.

In addition to the Wisdom traditions listed above, I have also benefited greatly from the teachings of the Enneagram, which also found me during my late twenties. While I reference it frequently in my writing, this is not an Enneagram book. The Enneagram is a comprehensive psycho-spiritual personality typing system that offers profound teachings on transformation, cultivating presence, and incorporating compassion into our relations with ourselves and others. I am a certified Enneagram educator, and I highly recommend that you use this tool to expand your self-awareness and find your unique growth path based on your personality. However, you don't need to know your Enneagram type to benefit from this book. If you want to find out more about the Enneagram, visit www.EnneagramInstitute.com or read one of the many wonderful books published on the subject.

CHAPTER 2:
What Is an Inner Critic?
Why Is Working with This Phenomenon Important?

We only perceive our malady when the cure begins.
—Archbishop François Fénelon

When I was a kid, biking down the street to the Little Dukes corner store to buy a pack of Big League Chew with my treasured allowance was a ritual of happiness. There was something so magical about that giant pack of gum and the attempt to shove all of it into my eight-year-old mouth at once that makes me crave it to this day. Not the gum, but the experience of drooling while chewing a wad of gum the size of a baseball, getting a sore jaw, laughing, and being careful not to choke. I could pick my nose in front of my older brother, Cory, at the same time; and no one cared, least of all me. That was back before I began hiding behind perfectionism. I was Felse, Cory was Craze, and everything was an adventure. Time slowed because our minds didn't race off to the past or the future. There was just this, giggles, and bubblegum. In the sloppiness of childhood, everything was perfect.

Growing older, I started to notice the wrongs of the world, that my nose gets cold when I play outside too long in winter, and that listening to Weezer's *Blue Album* won't actually fix my teenage angst forever. As I entered adulthood, I realized that you cannot get fresh coconut in Minnesota—and that if I did manage to get my hands on some, I had certainly polluted the Earth in demanding this fruit's long journey across thousands of miles. Humans became disappointing, spreading invasive and dangerous zebra mussels into our 10,000 Minnesotan lakes, gossiping behind one another's backs, perpetuating racism to and fro. Even I became disappointing. Despite good intentions, I allowed my integrity to slip. I held festering secrets, endlessly repeated unskillful habits, and hurt people I loved.

Oh to be young and free again, racing bikes as fast as our little legs could carry us down the alley; being an enlightened being, having no ego, no stake in image, and no judging or comparing voice inside the head. To be childlike once again, liberated from the Inner Critic, would bring the heart true peace and happiness. But alas, here we are: neurotic, broken, patterned adults, doomed to deal with our fate, our destiny of developing a personality. Our personality tends to become something we either adore and idolize or abhor and bemoan. Is there no other option? Are we to be stuck here forever, repeating our habits, hurting ourselves and our loved ones until the day that we die?

What about those asshole voices inside my head? Will they never leave me alone? There's the one that rips me and others apart for being less than perfect. Over time, I've come to call that voice Missy Prissy. She likes to say awful things like, *Ick. Those acne scars on your face are chasing away any chance of romance!* And what about the voice that constantly doubts my capabilities, inherent value, or belonging? (*Just stop trying. You're embarrassing yourself.*) Or the one that lures me into distraction and procrastination? (I call that voice Granny Divine, because she sounds so deceptively sweet.) Or the voice that convinces me I'll never have enough information, possessions, smarts, or charisma? That one is the Imposter Police, ready to pounce on me whenever it perceives that I'm getting too big for my britches, saying things like, *You really should get a few more degrees before putting yourself out there like that. Make sure you're ready for this so that people can take you seriously.* (You'll meet all these characters and others in the subsequent chapters.)

These are the thoughts and feelings that used to push me into depression, isolation, emotional repression, and frenetic activity, inwardly berating myself and lashing out at others. I reacted this way because I didn't know I had another option. I believed the voices in my head to be the Truth of who I was—

and, perhaps horrifyingly, even to be the voice of Godde. I never questioned the validity of the inner monologue; I just reacted to it. When I gave it any sort of conscious attention (while trying to meditate, for example), it was too much to bear because it confirmed my worst fears: that I was inherently flawed, corrupt, and broken beyond repair.

Does any of this sound familiar to you? Have you ever paid attention to what your internal dialogue is chattering about? If so, have you felt shame, fear, or irritation when listening to these thoughts? Have you ever tried to get the voices in your head to shut up by distracting yourself with busyness, television, food, drugs, alcohol, shopping, sleep, or even moving across the country?

Both these internal tapes and the emotional reaction to them are what I mean when I say "Inner Critic." Some other creative names I've heard for these voices are the Judge, the Tyrant, the Inner Committee of Assholes, Gremlins, Demons, the Crazy Lady in the Attic, and Brain Rats,[2] to name a few. (By the way, the music video for "Brain Rats" by Barbara McAfee is hilarious. Go watch it.) Once I started to pay attention to my inner dialogue, I realized there was a horde of competing voices vying for the last word. In the particular development of my personality habits, most of these voices were arguing about how quickly I should be executed for being a pathetic worm of a human. Either that, or they were pointing fingers at others to distract the jury from my crimes.

"We Are Legion"

Growing up Christian in a conservative Midwestern town, then studying theology at a progressive institution when I left home, I learned my Bible front to back and then forwards again. (Yes, that's how we say it in Minnesota: *forwards*. As in, "Then I says to him, 'Ain't nowhere to go but forwards.'") On the surface, it may seem that we are simple folk, but there's nothing simple about our culture of "Minnesota Nice." It's friendly smiles on top of layers of emotional repression, conflict avoidance, Catholic and Lutheran guilt, and panicked attempts to color within the lines.

BLESSING MY DEMONS

It recently occurred to me that the character I identify with the most in the Bible is a tortured, naked, demon-possessed man who lives in the cemetery next to a lake in the region of the Gergesenes. (Not my most flattering admission.) Although he had another name, the townsfolk knew him as Legion, because he was possessed not by one demon but by a whole battalion. Everyone was terrified of him, and they frequently chained him to the tombstones. The chains were no match for the demons, who repeatedly broke free so that Legion could get back to inflicting damage by cutting himself with sharp rocks.

Jesus and his friends decided to take their boat across the Sea of Galilee to offer teaching and healing to the people on the other side. Legion saw him approaching and came running out of the graveyard, shouting, "What do you want with me, Jesus, Son of the Most High God? In God's name, don't torture me!" The demons assumed Jesus was there to punish them.

Like this tortured soul described in Mark 5:1–20, I ran around frantically, trying to break my chains and cutting myself (figuratively, at least). Unlike Legion, who cut himself with stones, I cut myself with impossibly high standards, inner tirades, and a driving fear of making mistakes. I, too, had come to believe that the Big Man Upstairs was out to get me. Like Santa Claus carrying a big stick, he was kicking ass and taking names on his naughty list. And I certainly belonged on the naughty list. When I dared to take a glimpse into my mind, I could proclaim truthfully, "I am Legion, for we are many!" I am not only Chelsea; I also contain the voices of the stuck-up popular girl, the fire-and-brimstone preachers, the internalized Star Wars proverbs, and the maxims of my parents. I contain "demons" in the form of thoughts, feelings, and sensations of anxiety, dissociation, trauma, rage, criticism, depression, apathy, and various compulsions.

How horrifying. How confusing!

In this book, I have capitalized words that would not normally be used as proper nouns (e.g., Inner Critic, Demons, Shame Monster, Couch Potato, Street Preacher). It helps me to think of these aspects of my mental landscape as characters separate from myself so that I can more easily detach from them. Interacting with them in this way brings in a sense of curiosity and humor

WHAT IS AN INNER CRITIC?

that would otherwise not be possible. I can just tell them, "Thanks for your opinion, bro, but I got this one."

My first exposure to this method of working with the Inner Critic was through reading about Jesus's interaction with Legion. I am always amazed that Jesus tends to begin his interactions with people with a question. He doesn't assume he knows who they are, what they need, or what they want. In this particular case, he says to the slew of demons, "What is your name?" and proceeds to dialogue with them, asking them what they want and having mercy on them. My younger self always wondered why Jesus didn't just destroy them on the spot. Instead, he gives them permission to leave the tortured man and enter into a herd of nearby swine. Why?

I named this book *Blessing My Demons* instead of *Annihilating My Demons*. Why would we want to bless something that clearly causes so much pain? We will continue to explore this question throughout the book. But for now, I will say that this story of the man freed from the Legion of Demons is proof that Jesus was serious when he said, "Bless those who persecute you; bless and do not curse them" (Romans 12:14). He knew that throwing fire on fire never puts it out. Instead, he used the powerful tools of compassion, dialogue, curiosity, and openness to the possibility of options.

The Buddha, another of my beloved teachers, taught this as well when he said, "In this world hate never yet dispelled hate. Only love dispels hate. This is the law, ancient and inexhaustible" (Dhammapada 3–5). This law applies not only to our interactions with others, but also to how we relate to all the disparate pieces within ourselves that we'd rather be rid of. Tibetan Buddhism has developed a specific, imaginative, and very helpful practice around how to compassionately relate to our inner demons, called Chöd.[3] If Chöd is too new for you and you'd rather speak in familiar terms, there is a psychotherapy practice called Internal Family Systems[4] that deals with the acknowledgment and healing of the many parts within each of us. I tip my hat to both these traditions and teachings as I humbly present my version of "blessing my Demons."

Our Human Condition

While slowly making my way through a seminary in my late twenties, I worked for three years at a hip farm-to-table café in Minneapolis. The adrenaline rush of making almost three hundred beautifully presented espresso drinks in one brunch shift was exhilarating. The sampling of wares throughout the morning helped. So did dating the gorgeous, talented, creative, and kind line cook.

Just one problem: The cook was an alcoholic. Or was it a problem? At the time, I believed it was a habit I could easily help him cure.

I loved the roller-coaster ride we were on together. I was addicted to the excitement of dating addicts. Who wants a predictable, "normal" partner when you can wake up every morning not knowing what you're going to get? Maybe today it will be sweetness and intimate conversation. Or perhaps staging an intervention with his whole family. Or perhaps he will be carried into the house by his housemates because he passed out in the street before he could make it in the door. All these things were terrifying and enraging, but I stayed. I had committed. I needed to help him.

While in the throes of my full-blown codependency, one of my café coworkers lent me her copy of Eckhart Tolle's *A New Earth*. In it, he begins with a story of his first insight into the chaotic nature of the mind. In the midst of a deep depression, he found himself walking down the street behind an elderly woman who was incessantly talking out loud to herself, arguing back and forth about one thing or another. Tolle decided to eavesdrop on her conversation and continued to follow her. Somewhere along the way, it dawned on him that he was just like this old lady, with a constant stream of conversation going on inside his head. The only difference between them was that she verbalized it out loud, while he had chosen to keep the rants, arguments, worries, and justifications locked away in silence.[5]

This was a major revelation for me. If Eckhart Tolle also had Inner Voices and could pay attention to them with something amazing resulting from it (enlightenment!), then maybe I could face my Inner Voices with both courage and objective detachment as well. At least it wouldn't hurt to try.

WHAT IS AN INNER CRITIC?

By this point, I had developed quite the arsenal of defense mechanisms. I diverted my attention away from my pain by focusing on others. By teaching, helping, and resourcing my romantic partner, I could feel good about myself, valuable in some way. Self-righteousness was a go-to tool. So was giving him the "silent treatment" when I was angry at him for not meeting my high expectations. (This passive shaming technique is a family favorite.) I was also an expert at escaping reality by losing myself in fantasies, falling in love with some idealized future version of my partner or my life instead of facing the hard truth. I could see so much potential in him! Why couldn't he step into it? Above all, I made sure I could always put myself in a position of being *right*. I never entered an argument I couldn't win. I was constantly prepared to defend myself. All these habits were there for good reason: they had helped me survive my childhood.

Despite the persistence of my defenses, my Inner Critic still found ways to sneak past the ramparts: *You're a shitty girlfriend. He drinks because of you. How dare you think of leaving him alone in his suffering, you cold-hearted shrew. He's going to die, and it will be your fault! Then you'll be alone forever, because no one else will ever want you.*

Using my outdated defense mechanisms was no longer working. The Inner Critic was getting louder and more frequent. I felt my sanity slipping. All forms of self-care went out the window as I tried, with ever more desperation, to prove that I was good by saving my partner from his inevitable destruction. I was quickly spiraling toward a rock bottom that would, to my amazement, soon become a blessing.

When you hit bottom, there's nowhere to go but up. It supplies "the gift of desperation," as they so aptly say in Twelve Step programs. (Turns out this is another reason to bless the Demons. The pain they inflict can motivate us to snap out of our trance.) The suffering became unbearable, and I reached out for help. Finally, my illusion of stoic autonomy had been shattered. Fighting a wrenching pain in my gut, I worked up the courage to leave my partner. I loved him, but this perverse dance was killing both of us. Thankfully, I found my way to a Twelve Step program that is for the family and friends of alcoholics, where I began to loosen my grip on these outdated defense strategies and change my relationship with my Inner Critic.

Several years later, after countless hours of Twelve Step meetings, meditation, prayer, spiritual direction, therapy, Enneagram study, women's groups, and inner work retreats, I've gathered new tools to work with my Inner Demons and repair the havoc they have wreaked upon my life. I've come to learn that all of us have some version of an Inner Critic, and it doesn't make us bad people. It just makes us human.

What Is an Inner Critic, Exactly?

The Inner Critic is easy for some folks to identify because, for them, its voice is so harsh and jarring. (*You loser! No one will ever love you!*) For others, it is more sneaky, a subtle allurement into numbness, doubt, denial, inaction, or people-pleasing. (*What's the point? Why bother?*) However it shows up, the Inner Critic has but one purpose: to keep our ego from being hurt and from making moves that would be risky to our sense of self. The ego provides our sense of "me," and it is necessary for operating within healthy relationships and functioning well within society.

However, most of us (at least for a time) fall prey to the illusion that these personality traits, thoughts, feelings, and behavior are all that we are. We become attached to a certain way of being, largely because it has been working for us (in a way), keeping us comfortable, and helping us get what we want. For example, if my ego's sense of "me" is that I'm strong and in control, it protects me by making sure I don't expose my vulnerabilities and by driving me to exert my power over people and situations. Or, if my ego's story of "me" is that I'm defective and weak, I will find ways to attract others to my victimhood to get them to take care of me.

The deeper function of our personality is that it was developed in childhood as a series of defense mechanisms we learned to navigate our particular environment. These defense mechanisms become thought patterns, which can morph into our particular Legion of inner demons. Some of us escape childhood without acute trauma, but almost none of us reach our teen years without an Inner Critic that is alive and well. It's just a part of our natural development, at least in individualistic Western culture. How much of our particular flavor of Inner Critic is nature versus nurture is an ongoing debate, no matter to which psychological or spiritual system you ascribe. Trying to figure out what percentage of my personality is based on my culture of "Minnesota Nice" and how much arrived within my DNA will only get me lost in the weeds. It is the wrong question, at least if what we're shooting for is transformation and healing.

Let's not get it twisted. The personality, or ego, is not the problem. Imagine how boring life would be if no one had a personality—if we were all the same! It conjures up images of post-apocalyptic humans being controlled by robots. No, thank you. The problem is, when our superego, or the internalization of cultural rules, morals, and criticism (aka the Inner Critic), jumps into the fray and tries to keep us in the box of our personality, it removes our power of choice and flexibility. The superego reminds us of the ego's demands anytime we stray outside the box; and through various methods of poking and prodding, it coaxes us back into the safety of what is familiar.

Here's a simplified example: I'm walking down the street, eating a granola bar. When I finish, I have a choice: carry my trash until I find a garbage can, or throw it on the ground with all the other trash already in the neighborhood. No one would notice. The superego's pressure kicks in, telling me it would be wrong to litter. This was a value I was taught by my parents and elementary school teachers. Almost instantly, the Inner Critic chimes in with, *How could you even consider adding to the trash on the ground? You asshole.* It's trying to make sure I don't give in to my impulses and get in trouble. Thanks for keeping me in check, Inner Critic. But did you have to be such a jerk about it?

Here, it is important to distinguish the difference between the voices of guilt and shame. Guilt is that initial *ouch* we feel when we have done something harmful. It is a helpful reminder to not engage in that behavior again, like a one-time "note to self." Shame, on the other hand, convinces us not just that we have *done* something bad, but that we *are* bad. This voice tends to repeat itself in endless circles, becoming the tape that we can't shut off. Instead of thinking about the incident in a helpful way, we do all sorts of mental gymnastics to get the Shame Monster to shut up.

Nine Flavors of Inner Critic—Which Is Yours?

Michael Naylor and Lynda Roberts, two amazing teachers trained in the lineage of the Enneagram Institute, have together developed workshops and exercises on understanding the Inner Critic. In their workshop entitled Diving Deeper into Heart Healing, they look at the nine personality types through the lens of the Enneagram and have identified nine distinct flavors of Inner Critic and its demands. It will be helpful to name them here so that this explanation doesn't become too abstract. As you read these examples, notice which one makes you squirm the most or which one you take for granted as truth. When that happens, you've likely found your version of the Inner Critic! It might be uncomfortable, but don't freak out and run away. Stick with it. Stop and breathe if you need to.

There's a reason why you've picked up this book at this time in your life. It likely means you are ready, willing, and capable of looking at your interior landscape with some honesty and courage. It means you are ready to heal. It helps to remember that you are not alone in the ways you place demands on yourself. There is a whole club of people who are intimately engaged in a similar form of self-talk. So let's take a look at the nine types of Inner Critic and the particular demands they place upon us:

1. **You need to do what is right and make sure others also know what is right.** You need to be beyond reproach. And whatever you do, don't let your inner impulses lead you astray!

2. **You need to focus your attention on others so that you can help them.** You're selfish if you pay attention to your own needs. Just be nurturing and helpful!

3. **You need to develop yourself to be all that you can be.** You've got to be the best! Try harder so that you don't fail!

4. **You need to find your special and unique place in the world.** Your feelings are important, authentic, and unique to you. You need to follow your feelings!

5. **You need to explore, learn, and fill up your data bank with information.** You need to master something and figure things out. But you must not let your inner resources be drained!

6. **You need to be responsible and do what's expected of you.** Think ahead about what could happen, and be prepared. You need to get things done in a way that will satisfy others!

7. **You need to stay happy.** Get what you need to feel stimulated and satisfied, whether through experiences, material things, or relationships. Stay up and moving, and go after what you want!

8. **You need to be strong, powerful, independent, resourceful, and in control.** You're bad if you're vulnerable or weak! Be careful about showing sensitivity or needing the support of others.

9. **You need to keep yourself calm—and you can't have anger, because anger is aggressive.** You need to be sure that the people around you are okay. Just go along to get along. Chill!

On the surface, it may seem that any one of these is a great pep talk. What's so wrong with these beliefs? Well, pause for a moment and explore any one of these demands. Then imagine it being overdone, applied to every scenario, on repeat. Every day. For decades.

Take number 7 as an example. If I'm constantly chasing after the next exciting activity and only focusing on the positive, I will miss the depth and nuance of life. These "marching orders" encourage me to turn to external experiences to make me happy, which is a setup for disappointment and frustration. The circumstances of life are always changing, and nothing is permanent. This inner *demand* to stay happy will get me in the habit of running away from discomfort (both internally and externally) in an attempt to stay positive.

The problem is that all those painful feelings don't simply go away because I'm ignoring them. They get buried deep within me; and they fester, eventually bubbling to the surface in an overwhelming wave. My Inner Critic chimes in with, *Stop being such a downer! You'll bum everyone out! Don't feel sad, because you could become trapped in that feeling and never get out! Go cheer yourself up with a fancy dinner and start planning your next vacation!* I will then need more stimulating experiences to keep the grief, rage, and fear at bay. Addictions and distractions become the norm. Now we see how this seemingly optimistic strategy becomes a problem. A disaster, actually.

It's likely that every person can identify how all nine of these demands show up for them at various times. But for each of us, one of these voices will be the Master, the voice that trumps all the others. This is the area in which our Inner Critic will not let us slip—and if we do, there's internal hell to pay.

The ensuing internal hell can take many forms. I like to think about it through the metaphor of a prison cell. My cell is my personality, the particular box in which I feel, think, behave, and interact with myself and others. Even though it's cramped and often uncomfortable here, I've lived in this environment for most of my life. It is familiar, and therefore it brings with it a particular reassurance and stability. Why would I want to leave it to risk the Great Unknown? Besides, there is a prison guard at the door, ready to tase me if I transgress the boundaries. Is that pain worth the risk?

The guard is the Inner Critic, the gatekeeper. For me, an Enneagram One who identifies with the first set of demands, I get tased any time I feel like I've not acted out of integrity with my values and high standards. More often than not, the inner lashing comes as a result of *not* doing something, *not* speaking up to correct someone else's bad behavior, or the rare occasion when I give myself some time to rest (which my Inner Critic tells me is wasteful and irresponsible). As a reaction to this pain of offending the Critic, I either agree and feel shame ("Yes, I'm a bad person. Stupid Chelsea!"), obey it ("Since I took a ten-minute break, I'll make sure to work hard until 10:00 p.m. to make up for it!"), or fight back ("Shut up! I get to do whatever I want! I can't be the savior of the world!").

As soon as we engage in any way with the Inner Critic, it has already won. By agreeing, obeying, arguing, or justifying ourselves, we give validity to its voice. We give it ongoing permission to keep guarding our cell because we show that it has power over us. We get caught in a seemingly endless cycle of suffering. Yet we long for the freedom to leave the cage, have options, and find room to breathe. So what other options are there when we keep getting a lashing each time we try something new?

That is what the rest of this book will explore. We will look at ways the Inner Critic shows up and how to work with it in ways that break the cycle. Each chapter will give you stories and examples from my Inner Critic escapades, a cartoon illustration depicting each of my Inner Critic "characters," and reflection questions and exercises so that you can do your own work with your Demons. You can read the book straight through and then go back and do the exercises; or you can slowly make your way through, stopping for extended observation and reflection at the end of each chapter (which is what I recommend). The important thing is to engage with the exercises. You can always tailor them to your needs and translate any words that don't work for you.

The Three A's

There is a particular tool within Twelve Step communities that can be helpful to anyone embarking upon a journey to change patterns, beliefs, and habits. (That's you!) In a very real way, we are all addicted to our personality and our response to our Inner Critic. So the Twelve Step teachings on addiction have something to teach everyone. The tool I'm referring to is simply called the Three *A*'s. It is an acronym that stands for "Awareness, Acceptance, Action," which gives us an order of operations, a road map toward freedom.

In our work to make any type of change, the first step must be *awareness* of the problem or pattern. We must see it clearly and face it honestly. We must assess our role in the situation and not begin pointing fingers at others (e.g., "I'm only like this because my parents messed me up!"). Once we see or intuit that there is a problem, most of us want to jump quickly to *action* because we want it to be over and done with. We want to move on and get out of this discomfort. When we do that, we've skipped the magical ingredient of *acceptance*. It seems so counterintuitive, but it is the key to transformation.

My meditation teacher, Mark Nunberg, repeatedly uses this phrase in his talks: "It's like this now." If he had just said this once, or even ten times, the profundity of the statement would have been lost on me. By maybe the ninety-seventh time of hearing this seemingly dull expression, it sank into my psyche and I started to explore its deeper meaning: that *acceptance* is the way to freedom and peace, regardless of the present or past circumstances. Overanalyzing *why* I am the way I am and who is to blame is a fruitless exercise. The gold nugget lies in clearly seeing the way things are, without resistance. When I slowed down enough to observe my thoughts, there was an Inner Wisdom that broke through for just long enough to help me realize that my thoughts weren't my real identity. When I could observe my thoughts during meditation, using specific instructions on practicing mindfulness, I discovered there was some kind of spaciousness underneath that was closer to my True Self. In Zen, this is called the Big Mind. Enneagram teaching legend Helen Palmer calls this discovering the Inner Observer.

For me, that first split-second glimpse into freedom was both terrifying and cause for great hope. Terrifying because I had wasted so much time believing and reacting to my Inner Critic, and because I knew that change would require a lot of work and that things would never be the same. As scary as this was, it was still hopeful and enticing because it seemed there might be a way out of this pain. At least I had to try. Once Truth reveals itself, ain't nowhere to go but forwards.

Why Does This Type of Work Matter?

Inner work is important. It is not selfish or self-indulgent to work on ourselves, to believe that we deserve freedom from our demons. Dominant Western culture would have us believe that self-flagellation and self-hatred are the virtues of a humble soul. *They are not.* They only create wounds that we pass on to others. All this belittling and shaming of ourselves is covertly covered over by images of happiness. It's been engrained in us that happiness will come through material goods, youthful appearance, social status, and having the right partner and family. Ironically, the emphasis on these values tends to bring on more self-hatred and shame because we begin comparing ourselves to these models.

The teachings of Jesus of Nazareth are varied and profound, but I keep being drawn back to this proclamation: "I came so that you may have life, and have it abundantly" (John 10:10). Regardless of your beliefs of Jesus, if you live in the West, the culture of Christianity has likely affected you, for better or worse. The religion itself has wandered far from this encouragement toward abundant life. Shame and fear are often the tools of choice, but those are strategies that Jesus himself never employed. Abundant life—a life worth living, as illustrated by Jesus and all the great teachers—is not about wealth. Its fulfillment is due to an abundance of love, joy, generosity, compassion, equanimity, connection, and peace. These qualities are not possible when we are constantly berated and tased by the demands of an inner prison guard.

Unfortunately, there are no quick fixes for our psyche or soul. It took a long time for us to get into these habits of fear, shame, and self-criticism, so it naturally will take a long time to get out of them. If you thought this book would eradicate your Inner Critic by the time you got to the last page—sorry, it won't work like that. However, you *will* be well on your way to developing a flexible tool kit to deal with that pesky gatekeeper. You'll have discovered that there is hope for you, and we'll have some laughs along the way. Change is possible, and you are capable. For now, let it be enough to stay in that first *A* (awareness) without trying to fix anything about yourself. That will be a great start, and enough to begin an internal shift. The quote by Archbishop François Fénelon at the beginning of this chapter is a paradoxical encouragement. If we are not seeing our Inner Critic clearly, there is no hope for its healing. But as soon as we do see it, we're instantly on the path of awareness, which opens a world of possibilities. Only then can we begin to work on acceptance and action.

When we take the time to do our inner work, we have something beautiful to offer those around us. As long as we are constantly reacting to, pushing back against, or running from our Inner Critic, we will react to, push back against, or run from other people and our True Selves as well. Allowing the Inner Critic to be our Master limits our chances of true connection, intimacy, and love. And don't we all want more of that? Changing ourselves *is* changing the world, because what any one person does affects everyone around them. If we can plant seeds of serenity instead of fear, shame, and anger, imagine what kind of world is possible! This is not to say we can't simultaneously engage in the outer work in the world. The secret is that the inner work makes the outer work more effective!

So, for yourself, your family, your friends, your wider community, and the world, let's dive into this hard work together. May your Inner Critic work be blessed with the willingness, courage, wisdom, and serenity that you may find on the path to freedom. This is the same path that leads back to a healed Inner Child, happy to be a bubblegum-chewing, nose-picking, bike-riding maniac who knows how to let her True Self shine forth. After years of being shut down and covered up by the Inner Critic, your beautiful Inner Essence awaits.

WHAT IS AN INNER CRITIC?

STOP

The end of each chapter contains a series of Inner Work exercises. You will get much more out of this book if you do the exercises. Complete the exercises before you read on.

TAKE YOUR TIME.

It will be helpful to keep all of your reflections from these exercises in one journal so that you can easily reference them as you go on, since the exercises build upon each other.

YOUR TURN!
Inner Work Exercises

1. Brainstorm Names for Your Inner Critic

Set a timer for three minutes, then write down as many names for your Inner Critic (e.g., the Tyrant, the Taskmaster, the Shame Monster, Aunt Silvia, Her Majesty the Queen of Cynicism) as you can without an editing mind. Just keep your pen moving on paper. Get creative. It doesn't have to be "right." This is just a warm-up.

2. Find Your Flavor of Inner Critic

Work on your awareness of your Inner Critic and its specificities. Which number on the list of the Enneagram's Nine Flavors of Inner Critic feels the most familiar to you? Or the most nonnegotiable? It may take a while to find "the one," but pick one that feels alive right now and journal about it. In writing, reflect on these questions:

   a. How do these demands and beliefs show up for you?

   b. What were some times when you listened to these demands without question?

   c. Can you think of a time when you transgressed the set boundary and were hard on yourself as a result?

3. Observe Your Inner Critic's Demands

For the next week, engage in objective observation of yourself in relation to the internal demands you wrote about in the question above. Take five minutes before bed to reflect and jot down how this inner narrative put pressure on you that day. (Here's an example: *My Inner Critic's pressure on me to be nice and keep the peace stopped me from speaking up in the staff meeting today. I noticed I had a strong opinion that was different from the group, but I chose to remain silent because I knew it would make others uncomfortable. But the result is that now I feel uncomfortable!*)

Remember, these voices aren't personal. Just because you have an Inner Critic doesn't mean you are defective. It just means you are part of the human race. Welcome! Try to remain objective in your observations without attaching a value judgment (e.g., good/bad, smart/stupid, brave/cowardly). Try responding with curiosity instead of judgment or assessment. You can try out the response, "Oh, there's that Inner Critic again. How interesting!" instead of "Dammit, there's that Inner Critic again! I wish it would leave me alone!" Notice how your different responses make you feel afterward.

As we begin to pay attention to our inner landscape, it can be shocking, and it can feel like things are getting worse. They are not. We are simply noticing them more often through mindful awareness. We are just witnessing the activity in the mind that is constantly running its program in the background. Commit to being *gentle* with yourself throughout these exercises and observations. Gentle and brave.

PART 2
Tame It

CHAPTER 3:
My Two Masters, Vader and Yoda

You underestimate the power of the dark side.
—Darth Vader

When I was a kid in the '80s, I was obsessed with Star Wars before I had even seen the movies. Growing up without a TV in our household, Cory and I spent countless hours at the public library reading books and watching movies, trying to stay current on pop culture. While I was stuck downstairs in the kid section watching *Peter Rabbit*, Cory could watch "adult" movies upstairs (i.e., PG-rated films), where he discovered the magical wonders of a galaxy far, far away and recounted it to me during the car ride home. The two years of waiting to be old enough to meet Luke, Leia, Han, and Darth were torture. But the day finally came, and I was not disappointed.

I immediately loved the stark contrast between the light and dark sides, the tireless and valiant efforts of the rebels despite all odds, and the mysterious omnipresence of Lord Vader. He was terrifying not only because he could choke people from across the room, but also because he could get inside Luke's head from across the galaxy and speak dark allurements into his psyche. And I loved him for it.

Darth has always been my favorite character. Throughout the trilogy, we get glimpses into his past as Anakin, a normal boy trying to fight off his inner demons and not being quite clever or wise enough to do so. His inability to stave off the shadow within sunk in hard with me. Apparently, I learned, if you listen to your anger, you turn into a cosmic-sized megalomaniacal tyrant who oppresses whole planets and species and forever bows to a throne of pure and insatiable evil. In short, anger goes into the "bad" category. Check.

Three decades later, after doing some work around my Inner Critic, I quickly realized that, like with Luke Skywalker, Vader's voice also speaks dark yet sweet nothings into my ear. Darth was the first Inner Critic character that I easily identified and illustrated, and he is clearly the leader of my Legion. Just for fun, I've renamed him Harsh Grader. He shows up each time I make a mistake or approach the possibility of vulnerability, breathing down my neck in his iconic way (*ahh, brr . . . ahh, brr*). With him, the threat of failure feels like death. Just as it happened for countless Imperial officers, I'm afraid I'll hear him finally say, "You have failed me for the last time, Admiral Forbrook," and then I'll feel the crush of my windpipe and breathe my last breath.

When I first started studying mindfulness and meditation after college and heard, "You are not your thoughts—thoughts are just thoughts, and you don't need to listen to them," my head almost exploded. I instantly felt the stinging truth of this statement and the sweet freedom within. Stinging because I had wasted so much time believing Vader was the voice of God or Truth, and I'd experienced a taste of liberation in glimpsing a way out of this prison. If this new teaching was true, I would be free to try new things and fail, to make a fool of myself and still feel valuable, to relax back into the option of having *fun* and reacquiring a sense of humor. It's hard to have fun when vigilance against error is your constant companion. This teaching sounded too good to be true, but the seed had been planted. There were other, more spacious options waiting for me if I could dare the pain of looking truthfully within.

The other piece of Star Wars lore that I clung to, especially in my tween and teen years, was Master Yoda's teachings. (If, for some reason, you've made it this far in life without seeing these films, I'm sorry. I'll be done with the nerd references soon and move on.) Yoda's spirituality and that of the Jedi (aka the good guys) placed utmost importance on noticing what is going on in our mind and heart and *pushing away* emotions such as anger and fear that lead to corruption.

While there is some value in this teaching, I took it as absolute truth—and it has gotten me in quite a bit of trouble. Of course, Yoda wasn't the only one reinforcing this message for me. My family, my church, my friends, my teachers, my coaches, and all forms of media were pounding the same mantras into my head:

- "Only feel and express 'positive' emotions!"
- "Good people don't get angry, especially girls!"
- "If you believe in God and are still afraid or doubtful, your faith is weak!"
- "Aggression goes against Jesus's message of turning the other cheek, and it will likely lead to sexual deviancy."

(Wait, what? It turns out that, in conservative Midwestern culture, practically anything is a slippery slope toward sexual deviancy. But that's a story for another chapter.)

I recognize that not everyone internalizes messages like this with such enthusiasm. There is certainly an element of contextual culture at play, as well as my personality's innate tendency to latch on to all-or-nothing thinking as a sense of security. It reassures me to put things into categories of right and wrong and to then align myself with the good guys. This is my particular flavor of perfectionism (of which there are many flavors, by the way!). I just happened to latch on to the compulsion to do and be *good,* even at my own expense.

The other teaching of Master Yoda that I latched on to as my motto and repeated incessantly to friends and family was, "Do or do not. There is no try." He suggests that if young Skywalker truly believes he can lift a spacecraft with his mind, he will. (Due to these impossible standards, I've started calling him Master High Barr.)

Similarly, Jesus of Nazareth apparently said this to his disciples after they had failed to exorcise a demon: "Because of the littleness of your faith you have failed; for truly I say to you, if you have faith the size of a mustard seed, you will say to this mountain, 'Move from here to there,' and it will move. Nothing

will be impossible for you" (Matthew 17:20). So if I fail, it means I don't have enough faith? Then it's best to stick to things I'm certain to succeed at.

Bingo! I had found my motivation: avoidance of failure and mistakes. This is not, I'm sure, what either Yoda or Jesus had intended, but it was too late. My interpretation grew legs, solidified. I believed that nothing was worth doing if I couldn't do it perfectly. Being *good* meant being prepared, well-studied, clear-minded, correct, and ready to perform without flaw. Not having complete control of my mind, emotions, and impulses meant I fell into the unspiritual pool of common sinners. Failing Master High Barr meant failing Jesus . . . or something like that. I'm sure you can see that these high standards were a setup for disappointment, self-hatred, and shame. This attitude showed up literally *everywhere* in my life.

I remember the very first time I felt the sting of imperfection. I was in first grade, and I was playing with a friend in the classroom. We were under an easel during playtime, in the blissful world of imagination (probably experiencing ourselves as wild animals or ninjas), when I suddenly realized my teacher was shouting my name—loudly, and with a frustrated tone. My heart sank. Somehow I hadn't realized that everyone else had cleaned up and was sitting back on the rug, crisscross applesauce. I had gotten sloppy, lost myself in joyful spontaneity. And there was Harsh Grader, softly yet ominously breathing in my ear (*ahh, brr . . . ahh, brr*). Never again would fun trump obedience and order. At that moment, my Inner Critic started gaining power. I trusted it to help me remain vigilant, to stay out of trouble.

And it did just that. Sort of.

The second time the perfection monster bit me in the booty was probably a year later. I was drawing at the table at home, which was one of my favorite pastimes. My favorite subject matter was animals, but that day I was trying to sketch a person. My dad walked by to check in on my progress. With what I am now sure was gentleness and love, he offered me some constructive criticism.

"His arm looks like a noodle," he said with a slight chuckle, surely trying to bring some levity to the comment.

It didn't work. I stopped breathing.

"Make sure you show a sharper bend at the elbow so you can tell he has bones in his arm," my dad went on to say.

Ahh, brr. Ahh, brr. Surely any moment I would drop dead.

Up until this point, I had received nothing but compliments for my artistic endeavors. But that day, I was crushed. I had tried something new and failed. I had let Yoda down. How humiliating that I hadn't noticed this feature of human bodies at age eight! Never again would I present my work to the world until it was at its best. Never again would I show my messy, unfinished process. Never mind that my classmates were still drawing stick figures. They were lazy, with low standards. Comparing myself to them brought me no comfort, as the only thing that mattered was the high bar I had set for myself.

Interestingly enough, this did not cause me to quit drawing. Instead, it coaxed me behind closed doors until the finished, perfected project was ready to be presented. This one little mistake—this one tiny critique—drove me to step up my game, practice my technique relentlessly, and produce incredibly realistic drawings. In this scenario, my Inner Critic was producing a positive outcome. (Sometimes the Inner Critic is helpful like that, which can make it difficult to discern when it's speaking the truth or crossing a line.) Cory and I had a folder filled with meticulously detailed drawings of Star Wars characters, among other subjects. I got to the point in high school where I started dreaming of becoming an artist.

One morning in eleventh grade, during a visit to my dermatologist, the doctor asked me what I wanted to be when I grew up. I hesitated. Could I try sharing the truth of my dream? I was already in the vulnerable position of having an old man scrutinize the acne on my face, shove me under sun lamps, and dope me up with tetracycline to try to make me more beautiful. As if my Inner Critic wasn't already having a field day about my failure to meet the beauty standards of our culture! (A few years later, I discovered I could have just taken birth control pills to balance out my hormone levels, which were the cause of the acne. But that would have been just one more slippery slope to a life of fornication, so it obviously wasn't an option presented to me by the circles in which I moved.)

For whatever reason (probably because I liked the old man), I blurted out the truthful answer to his question. "I want to be an artist."

"An artist?" the dermatologist answered. "No, no, no. You're way too smart for that. With your grades the way they are in math and science, you should become a doctor, like my daughter. Besides, you can't make a living being an artist anyway. You'll starve."

Ahh, brr. Ahh, brr.

And that was that. With such an authoritative voice assuring me the chances of trying and succeeding as an artist were slim to none, I changed course. My parents, God bless 'em, would have supported me if I had wanted to go to art school. That's just who they are. My whole life long—even when they've disagreed with my choices, my lifestyle, my politics, or my chosen romantic partners—they have kept their mouths shut and loved me just the same. But Dr. What's-His-Face had spoken. That door was shut. The outer critic had worked its way in. *Note to self,* the Inner Voices told me. *Practicality and taking a sure path is the way to go if you are going to attain perfection and success. Stick with what feels safe. Can't do no good in the world if you're starving.*

You'd think these harsh and childish interpretations of reality would have left me as soon as I reached adulthood. Quite the contrary: Those seeds had been watered enough times over my formative years that they had grown deep roots into my neural pathways. My mind had thought those thoughts ten million times, and the ruts had been created. I now know there is no shame in this, as we all have our idiosyncrasies, neurotic tendencies, and unskillful patterns that keep us imprisoned. But back then, I wondered why I couldn't just be spontaneous, brave, and free. What was wrong with me?

Once safely through the codependent and perfectionistic mayhem of my twenties, Harsh Grader's grip on my spirit began to loosen. I was learning to recognize his misguided mentorship, to just observe the feeling of imminent death and watch it eventually pass. I needn't react compulsively to his demands; I could just observe them and make different choices. For years, I had believed there was something inherently broken, bad, and corrupt within me. Strangely, introducing some awareness into the equation has done wonders.

Simply observing and naming my Inner Tyrant has taken away his power on my good days.

This shift started happening because I was committing to the practice of mindful meditation, as well as living a life guided by the Twelve Steps. I was voraciously consuming books from spiritual teachers who offered an alternative view in contrast to the demanding religion of my youth (and of the Jedi). Eckhart Tolle, Thich Nhat Hanh, Lois W., and Richard Rohr were teaching me how to be kind to myself, to respect myself, to live in the present moment without resistance.

Another surprising thing happened too. When I drew a picture of my Inner Critics, Harsh Grader and Master High Barr, they suddenly became humorous! Before they were on paper, they were running my life, completely terrifying. I was identifying with them and felt oppressed by their standards. But once they were drawings, I realized they were actually kind of cute. I suddenly felt some distance from them, like they were separate from me. I also felt I could safely dialogue with them or choose to tune them out, because they were so absurd! Bringing them fully into the light through a cartoon drawing helped me see them for what they are: not real. A figment of my imagination.

Before I acknowledged the existence of my inner Vader, I was spending so much energy trying to deny and repress my anger and aggression. Whenever I turned a blind eye by trying to pretend I was happy and in control of my impulses all the time, fooling others but never myself, the Sith Lord only gained power. (That's Vader, for all you non-nerds.) He had growing evidence that I was no longer meeting my job description. I was constantly being blackmailed by the Inner Critic with thoughts like, *If you mess this one up, I swear to God I will tear you to shreds!* It was exhausting, being so buttoned up and put together all the time.

Unfortunately, just knowing this isn't enough to make the inner tyrant disappear altogether. A few years ago, after identifying and drawing my Harsh Grader, I was on my way to a gathering at my friend Ryan's house. I had been there a few times before, so I chose to run out the door without checking Google Maps. I knew it was somewhere around 24th and Blaisdell Avenue, so I hopped on my bike with enough time to arrive five minutes early. When I got there, things weren't looking quite right. So I biked a few blocks north and realized this was too far. I turned around and biked several blocks to the south. Where was that damn YMCA by his house?

My blood pressure was starting to rise. I was going to be late. I turned around again and went farther this time. When I came to Franklin Avenue, it hit me like a ton of bricks: *It's 34th and Blaisdell, not 24th! Dammit!* All hell broke loose within me. I had committed an unforgivable sin—being late—and I was now in a rage.

As I biked as fast as I could back toward Ryan's place, the Inner Judge berated me the whole way: *How could you be so fucking stupid! You've been there a zillion times. You've lived in this city for a decade! How could you possibly screw this up? You are such a moron! "Oh, sorry I'm late, everyone. I got lost in my own neighborhood because I'm a total failure." Bike faster, you idiot!*

One thing about the Inner Critic is that it has no shame. I would never in a million years say words like this to anyone else but myself. While locking up my bike outside Ryan's apartment, my friend Curtis was getting out of his car and meandering his way toward me in a completely relaxed manner. This set off the Inner Critic again: *Fuck you, Curtis! You're late too! How can you be so calm?* When the voice violates my principles and integrity by turning on others, I know I'm in deep. I was so mad at myself that I was shaking. It felt like I had just taken sixteen shots of espresso and my heart was ready to explode. (*How could you have been so stupid, you dumbass!*)

That's the other thing about the Inner Critic. Like a broken record, it loves to repeat itself.

In a moment of vulnerability, I shared my Inner Critic attack with Curtis, because I love and trust him. And like the angel he consistently is, he calmly said, "Wow, you're being really hard on yourself. I don't think you're stupid at all; I think you temporarily got turned around. I'm late all the time. It doesn't make you a bad person." By the time he finished, I was crying, because being confronted with calm compassion was such a shocking contrast to what was happening inside me. "C'mon, we'll go in late together," he said, putting his arm around me.

It took about forty minutes for my body to stop having a physiological response to my Inner Critic attack. But Curtis's kind words had snapped me back into reality, and I could enter the room, name my present struggle out loud to a few other friends, and set the cognitive pattern aside. With mindfulness, I could be present to my other friends and their sharing while remaining a compassionate presence to my poor nervous system. When near-death experiences present themselves (and since I have an inner Harsh Grader, something as small as getting lost could be cause for termination), we go into a fight-flight-freeze response. My tendency often is to fight, despite my good-girl narrative. It's just my wiring; I suppose my limbic system evolved this way.

There is also a much more practical explanation for why I was so triggered by such a trifling matter: childhood conditioning. I remember our family getting ready for church every Sunday morning and leaving with plenty of time to spare so that we could be seated in our pew ten minutes before the service started. We never missed a Sunday. Even when we were away for the weekend camping, we'd go into town and find a church to attend.

But one Sunday was different. We were scrambling to get ready, running behind. I'm not sure what threw us off schedule, but my father was visibly distressed. His body was tense, and his speech was curt as he tried to round us up. There was no talking during that car ride. We knew we were in trouble. We knew that silence was a sure sign of wrath. When we pulled into the church parking lot, we were what other families would consider to be right on time, at 9:00 a.m. "We're turning around," was all my dad said before we drove back home.

In the silence, I could feel him roiling inside. I knew he couldn't bear the embarrassment of us walking in and finding our seats while the first hymn was already being sung. Someone would see us sneaking into the back row. *Shame.* I spent the rest of the day walking on eggshells, afraid my father's love would be removed from me forever. Apparently, that stuck with me. Lateness equaled disconnection from those you love.

One of the most important things I've learned from my meditation teacher, Mark Nunberg at Common Ground Meditation Center, is that our reactions to things are not personal. They are just nature expressing itself. I respond this way because of everything that has come before; all the cumulative thoughts, actions, and experiences I'd had led me to that moment. It could be no other way. But unlike Master High Barr's pseudo-Zen teachings, this does not mean that the dark path will dominate my destiny forever if I give in to a moment of rage. At any given moment, we are presented with a choice. With mindfulness, we can introduce a sacred pause between stimulus and response. Now that I know there are other ways of being and responding, I have a responsibility to choose them. (Just as Vader did when he redeemed himself by saving his son and returning to Love before taking his last breath. It's never too late to change! *sobs*)

While I couldn't stave off the initial attack of my Inner Tyrant during that bike ride, I did not allow it to consume me for the rest of the evening. Instead, I recognized it for what it was: an Inner Critic attack that was not personal. I ended up having a good time with my friends. In my twenties, that Inner Critic attack would have gone on for weeks, maybe years. I used to believe that if I beat myself up first, it will prevent others from doing so and prevent me from making the same mistake again. And the longer the beating, the more effective I believed it will be. More harshness would lead to more self-control, which would lead to less opportunity for outside scrutiny.

This has never proven to be effective. Over time, I began to get sick of these inner lashings. They seemed to only make me feel worse about myself. It caused me to tighten up on my emotional repression and self-control, which led to more reactive responses to perceived failings. It was a cycle of misery. So it was time for Harsh Grader to retire. While he had been helpful with some things, like getting good grades and producing quality work, I decided to write him a termination notice and break it to him as gently as possible:

Dear Harsh Grader,

Thank you for your thirty-plus years of dedicated, thorough, tireless work. No one but you could have persevered so continuously, working so much overtime, never using your vacation or sick days for three straight decades. Your commitment to this work is astounding.

Over the years, you have driven me to succeed in so many ways. You have pushed me so hard, protecting me from outside criticism, from the pain of failure and ridicule. I know your intentions have been good from the start and that you only wanted the best for me. I thank you for that. I am who I am because of you.

After more than three decades of diligent service, I award you your retirement. Don't worry about me. I've got plenty of other voices on my committee who are here for me. My Higher Power has got my back. Finally, it's time for you to take a much-needed vacation. Go ride your motorcycle cross-country. Play endless rounds of golf in Scottsdale. Lie on the beach and enjoy several rounds of Long Island ice teas with an extra slice of lemon. Get in touch with your inner Anakin. You can come back and visit if you get lonely—as long as you don't sneak in the back door to try to take charge. I insist that you don't do another full day's work. For your own good.

Peace be with you, my friend. Your motorcycle awaits.

Much love,
Chelsea

YOUR TURN!
Inner Work Exercises

1. Draw Your Inner Critic

Think about the last time you were beating yourself up, feeling down about yourself, or driving yourself to be better, more, or the best. Got one? Congratulations! You've identified an Inner Critic attack! Now, jot down a few of its favorite phrases. What does it love whispering or shouting at you? Are there any names it loves calling you repeatedly? (Perhaps *dummy*, *worthless*, *lazy*, or *asshole*?) Write those down. If you're stuck, go back to Exercise 2 from the previous chapter and look at what the Inner Critic loves to demand of you.

Next, close your eyes and imagine what this Inner Critic looks like. It might be silly, terrifying, a clearly defined character, an animal, a weather pattern, or a nebulous presence. Perhaps it's your mother's voice—or your childhood priest! Whatever comes to you is the right image. Just go with it. Enjoy the process. Even have fun with it!

Then, make a sketch of this particular Inner Critic, including its main messaging, words, and phrases. You don't need to be a great artist to do this. A rough sketch will do. Perhaps a certain setting comes along with it, or a tone of voice, a theme song, or a smell. Invite all your senses into this imaginative exploration.

The objective here is to gain more comfort and confidence in interacting with this Inner Critic voice. Right now, we are not trying to get rid of it; we're just getting to know it. Notice if anything shifts inside you after you see a visualization of this character. For now, let the noticing be enough.

Good job! You've identified and named your first Inner Critic character.

2. Contact the Quiet Mind behind the Scurrying Mind

As we move forward on this journey of detaching from our Inner Critic, we must connect with a part of ourselves that is more authentic. There is a part of us that is deeper, more true, and more essential to who we are than the ever-changing thoughts in our heads. Our thoughts are actually quite trivial and mostly irrelevant to who we really are. We can begin to distinguish between our Ego (where the Inner Critic hangs out) and our Essence, which is the space within us from where wisdom, guidance, value, and serenity arise. Try this short exercise to begin disidentifying from your Ego and your Inner Critic.

   a. Set a timer for five minutes, and get in a comfortable position.

   b. Close your eyes or soften your gaze. Turn your attention to your breathing. Relax your body.

   c. Begin to notice your thoughts as they pass through, without getting caught up in the content of the thoughts. Gently label each thought with the word *thinking*, then return to your breath.

   d. After a couple of minutes, turn your attention to the quiet spaciousness *between* your thoughts and *behind* your thoughts. Without trying to grasp this calmness in the mind, become aware of it.

   e. Drop the question, "Who or what is noticing my thoughts?" Sit with this question without striving for a concrete answer.

As you come out of this exercise, jot down your observations in your Inner Work Journal. How would you answer that last question? What is really *you*? Are there different parts of you? Which part feels alive and free? Which part feels constricted and stressed? Which part have you been identifying with? Which part would you *like* to identify with?

CHAPTER 4:
Missy Prissy

That's why her hair is so big: it's full of secrets.
—Damian, portrayed by Daniel Franzese in *Mean Girls*

I was depressed during my junior year of high school. I was also angry as hell. Cory had left home for military boot camp, and I felt so alone. To top it off, Lucas, the pigtail-wearing artist and love of my life since fifth grade, was now dating my childhood best friend, Bethany. It was a slap in the face. That backstabber! It was quite surprising too, like when you overturn one of those disgusting, plump, white grubs in the garden. You want to squish it, but you're too scared to touch it. So you quickly cover it up and pretend you never saw it. (I'd heard Lucas and Bethany were having sex, too.)

My drum set in the basement helped a bit. Banging out "Purple Haze" was at least some reprieve from the loneliness. In this game of Boys Chase Girls, Girls Chase Boys, no one ever really won. It was like a never-ending game of Chutes and Ladders, where I just kept sliding back down every time I was close to the finish line. Anger engulfed me and my thoughts: *Frickin' Bethany, man. She knows I've loved him for seven years! And even more unbearable, now my brother/best friend has left home at the worst possible time. He's probably going to die too, since some radical terrorists just flew their damn planes into some buildings in New York City. War is inevitable with all these stupid people in charge. We're probably all going to die. I hate everyone!*

The pressure was building, the temperature rising. There were nights when I'd go and sit out under the big tree in our front yard during a raging June thunderstorm and scream as loud as I could whenever a thunderclap shook the earth. A small part of me hoped I'd get struck by lightning. Another part of me was terrified of the storm. But that was why I loved it. It made me feel alive and mortal.

I wondered if my parents knew I was depressed. I did my best to cover it up by becoming an explosive ball of rage around them, then hiding in my room reciting the lyrics to Weezer's "The World Has Turned and Left Me Here," wiring my brain into pessimism and hopelessness. I remember that they took me out to Dairy Queen after Cory left to try to console me, and I just sat there, silent and fuming. Dad would try to help me with my calculus homework, and I'd throw a complete tantrum as soon as I didn't understand something. I would even snap at Mom over any little thing:

- "Ugh! These peas are mushy."
- "I need my red polyester pants tomorrow! Why haven't you washed them yet?"
- "Do you have to dress like that in public? You're embarrassing."

I was a real charmer. A total sweetheart.

Meanwhile, another phenomenon had developed: Darth Vader had found an unlikely friend. The cast of characters inside me was growing, and another voice was vying for the upper hand. Although I didn't acknowledge or name her until fifteen years later, this was another Inner Critic who began to turn her judgment on others to avoid the pain of her imperfection. Her name was (and still is) Missy Prissy, and she's a Class A bitch. I've made it a point to never use that offensive word about women *ever*, but it's the quickest and surest way to describe this voice in my head.

Before I go on, I must say that Missy Prissy is the part of me that I'm most ashamed to share. When sharing my Inner Critic drawings with friends, I would briefly let them glance at this one, then turn the page before they could read the horrible things going through her head. Thankfully, a few things have changed that allowed me to move from humiliation to humility around this part of me. The first, which I learned from many Buddhist teachers, is that thoughts are just thoughts; they are not who we are. Just because I have bitchy thoughts doesn't mean that I *am* a bitch. The mind will continue in its conditioned thinking as long as we are not paying attention. As soon as we start to pay attention, we realize that there is a part of the mind that is spacious and clear that can *observe* the thoughts. In observing my horrendous and constant stream of judging thoughts, I was given instructions on how to begin detaching from them. Instead of fighting against them or feeding them, I learned to just note that judging was happening and then let that thought float on its merry way.

You ordered that for lunch? (Judging.)

I'm feeling embarrassed for her. (Judging.)

The second lesson that gives me faith that sharing these Inner Critics will be helpful to me (and maybe even to others) is that naming and sharing these parts of ourselves deprives the Inner Critic of its power. There's something almost magical about it. Naming it and admitting it to myself is one level, but saying it out loud to another person is quite another. There is a release, a weight that comes off one's shoulders. I know that when my friends have demonstrated this type of vulnerability, it gives me permission to do the same. Perhaps making this dirty little secret public won't kill me after all. (I also dare to put Missy Prissy in here so that you feel better about yourself. There's no way your Inner Critic is as awful as mine!)

Yet another thing that encourages my honesty around this is that I've learned our Inner Critic voices are really just strategies for survival. They're defense mechanisms that helped us survive and navigate our particular upbringing. Knowing this takes away the feeling that this is somehow *personal*. It is not. Missy Prissy is not me. She is just a set of habits and well-worn neural pathways. Modern brain science around neural plasticity tells me that she can be undone.

So without further ado, I introduce you to this (particularly embarrassing) defense mechanism. She may not *look* like a demon, but she is every bit as insidious and twisted as Harsh Grader.

If you laughed at any of Missy's tirades—good job! The only way these Inner Critic voices are tolerable is if we bring some humor to them. Otherwise, it's just depressing. Anyone who knows me will find this character funny, because she appears to be so contrary to the way I present myself. I've always been tomboyish, always sweaty from my bike commute, without makeup and with dirty fingernails from digging in the garden. And yet, there she is, in all her Mean Girl glory, my annoyingly consistent companion.

Not surprisingly, Missy tends to focus on people's appearances. In Brené Brown's book *Daring Greatly,* she talks about the number one shame trigger for women and for men. For women, it is our looks, our bodies, and our attractiveness measured up against impossible, photoshopped standards. For men, it is being perceived as weak.[6] What a bummer.

A couple of years ago, while on a silent retreat, I wrote down all the self-deprecating thoughts I was having about myself. When I sat back and looked over the list, I thought to myself, *Holy shit. These are all things that my mother nitpicks me about!* In the very next breath, I realized, *Holy shit! These are also the things my mother beats herself up about!*

My head was spinning. This whole time, I had thought I had invented these judgments: too skinny, too fat, too loud, too quiet, too showy, too stupid. In that moment, I realized that I was just parroting back what had been modeled to me. Tears began to stream down my face as I saw all these same patterns of criticism in my maternal grandmother. Where had Grandma learned to berate herself and others this way? The same places we all do: the magazine covers; the Hollywood standard of beauty; the narrative about what it means to be a good girl, a good Christian lady, a good wife. For the first time, it sunk into my bones in a visceral way that none of this is personal. We are all just sponges, soaking up the garbage we are swimming in. As Bob Dylan sings in his song "Brownsville Girl," "If there's an original thought out there, I could use it right now."

Once I started seeing these thoughts clearly, I began to notice them in real time, as they were happening. At first, my reaction to this was to judge myself for judging others. (*Stop it, you asshole! Why can't you just be nice? You're such a horrible person!*) The result was shame, then further judgment for being so sensitive. Around and around I'd go, in a quick spiral down the shitter. When Jesus said, "Do not judge or so you shall be judged" (Matthew 7:1), I don't believe this was some sort of warning about our entry ticket into heaven. I believe he meant it in a much more practical and immediate sense. When I judge others, I instantly judge myself. My conscience appropriately kicks in and feels the *ouch* of that judgment. The Inner Critic pounces on the Self the same way it pounces on others. It is this instant cause and effect that Jesus warns us against.

At some point, I realized that the reactionary voice with which I judged Missy Prissy was just another version of Missy: mean-spirited, without an ounce of compassion. The same would happen with Darth. When he was breathing down my neck over the fear of making a mistake, my response was to double down even further into perfectionism. But we will never heal our wounds and patterns by employing the same strategies against them. We need a new strategy.

My friend Gabe once told me, "That painful feeling after making a mistake is actually a gift." He went on to explain that in allowing ourselves to feel that painful reverberation in our heart, we take in the consequences of our misstep, therefore opening the space to learn from it and choose differently next time. It is when we allow the Inner Critic to attach a story to this mistake or judgment (e.g., *Stupid Chelsea, you're such a judgy asshole!*) that we lose the natural intelligence of our conscience.

When I started practicing responding to myself—and to Missy—in a more compassionate tone, she began to diminish. I distinctly remember this moment six years ago, as I was watching a woman struggle down the street in her stilettos, and this foreign thought slid through my mind: *That poor woman. Her feet must really hurt.*

This might not sound revolutionary to you. But to me, it felt like fireworks exploding in my head. You see, this was exactly the type of person I loved to hate. My typical thoughts would have been, *What an idiot. Doesn't she know that by wearing those ridiculous things, she is upholding the patriarchy, making women look weak and vulnerable? How could she possibly run away if she were attacked? I have no sympathy for your self-inflicted pain that is clearly driven by your lack of self-esteem!*

So you now see why this new and spontaneous thought of kindness toward this woman almost knocked me off my feet. I was giddy with excitement: *There is hope for me! Perhaps I'm not a piece of shit after all. Hallelujah!* I practically skipped the whole way home. I felt so proud and loving. And, I dare say, I felt a glimpse of self-love for the first time since early childhood. Therein lies the immediate impact of kindness toward others: It leaves a beautiful aftertaste in the heart and mind. Its pureness begins to give us hope for redemption. Once we experience it, there is a wholesome desire to get some more of where it came from. The snowball effect begins its momentum in a new direction.

But that momentum didn't just magically start on its own. It took clarity of intention and a willingness to invest time into my psychological healing. There are many ways to do this. For me, it took working several methods simultaneously for years before I felt like I was approaching something resembling "healthy" and "loving." But there were shifts and wonderful surprises along the way that kept me motivated to keep going.

I began by meeting with a spiritual director regularly. While I didn't know this was happening at the time, I now know that it was Janet's loving and accepting witnessing of me in all my mess that helped me become open to loving and accepting myself. I told her everything because she felt safe. The space to be vulnerable with another human was profoundly healing. And I was willing to be honest and open to changing.

I've also met with a couple of therapists along the way, with similar results. Meeting with my Twelve Step friends every Tuesday night was also a practice in exposing my doubts, fears, rage, and insecurities to others. I talked openly about the pressures put on me by my Inner Critic, and so did others. I discovered I wasn't alone, and the weight of shame began to lift. Alongside these practices, I learned to meditate (a way of paying attention to my thoughts without being controlled by them) from knowledgeable teachers, both in person and through reading books on meditation. I learned about the Enneagram, which further clarified the unique structure of my inner world and the particular demands of my Inner Critic so that I knew what to watch out for. All of this helped me to slowly begin changing my behaviors and thoughts, which changed my feelings about myself to be more positive. I learned to act in a way that made it easier for me to respect myself.

If all of this sounds like too much work, you're right! When we think about all the things that need to be done to truly change and heal, it's overwhelming. The key is to just start somewhere, pick something, and do it. Stick with it. Remain open, and trust that the next right thing will arrive at just the right time. If that sort of trust sounds impossible for you, it's okay to just "act as if" you trust the process. In the beginning, that's enough to get you on the path. It won't take much time for you to experience a positive shift, even if it's a small one; and that will provide you with faith to stay the course. But that won't happen if you sit around waiting for a sure thing, trying to gather all the evidence that a certain practice will work for you. The evidence comes from *doing*, not thinking. Chances are your heart is already calling you toward what is good for you. *Listen.* And then put it on your calendar.

When I had that new thought about the woman in heels, the mysterious thing about this split second of compassion was that I didn't try to force it. It just flowed through me without trying, without any self-will. In a sense, this loving capacity within me wasn't "me" either. It just felt like a moment of grace, where I was allowed to tap into the universal stream of Love. While this moment was a pure gift, I also know that it could not have happened without the awareness and interrogation practices I had begun to engage in with my Inner Critic—practices I had learned from spiritual direction, the Enneagram, therapy, meditation, and Twelve Step work over the last decade. This curiosity and faith that I could change opened up a space in my heart to allow the Love to find some room to flow. It bubbled up like a pure spring from deep within, an ancient pureheartedness that had been tamped down by years of judging myself and others. At long last, Grace was allowing me some relief from the prison of my personality.

Having had a small taste of freedom, I continued to immerse myself in teachings around changing habits, thought patterns, and healing the wounds of personality. If we are sponges soaking up the water around us, we need to intentionally immerse ourselves in clean water to have any sort of positive change occur. I began choosing my friends more carefully and spending more time with people who were kind, caring, and self-aware. I began to learn from their example how to communicate honestly and openly, from a space of compassion. These friends pointed out to me when I was being too hard on myself and holding myself to inhuman standards. I continued to seek out older mentors and spiritual guides who could help me through the deep and tangled thicket of my mind and heart. I relished the support of my recovery community, where I began sorting out my Inner Critic's habit energies from the pure innocence and goodness still alive deep within me. The waters around me were starting to clear; and slowly but surely, I began to heal and let go of my Inner Critic's stories.

Even after beginning on the path of self-awareness and healing, the Inner Critic is persistent in trying to maintain the upper hand. She creeps in whenever mindfulness slips away, whenever you are least expecting her. Any little thing can set her off, even when you're in the midst of pleasant circumstances.

One morning, I woke up in the woods of northern Wisconsin and was shocked to see a red fox right outside the cabin window. Even more extraordinary was that the fox was following immediately behind a white-tailed deer, and the two of them were relaxed and seemingly comforted by each other's presence. They moved about the forest together slowly, easefully.

How had this unlikely pair hooked up? They made me jealous in a way, since they looked like they had always had a friend by their side, navigating life's twists and turns with them, making choices together in an unspoken secret language between them. I wanted that in a mate. Regardless of how different we might be on the outside, I fantasize to this day that we'll have this deep understanding of each other, communicating without words.

Alas, the sport of courtship is a competitive one. There are winners and losers when it comes to romance, and I often seem to be on the losing end. Why can't my teenage heartthrob Jonny Lang just come down off the stage and tell me he's sick of stardom and ready to settle down with me to a simple Midwestern life? These thoughts are like a continuous drizzle that clouds the otherwise sunny country of my soul. Unfortunately, wild and fantastical thinking won't get me back in the dating game. Those thoughts are about as useful to me as studying exoplanets: interesting and alluring, but I'll never get there in this lifetime. So what's the point?

This fog of self-pity naturally leads me to begin judging others. It's too painful to hang out over here, judging myself for being alone, and then judging myself for judging myself: "Jeez, Chelsea, what kind of feminist are you? There's nothing wrong with being single! It's prime time to practice self-care, self-sufficiency, and self-awareness!"

"Yeah, maybe. . . . But where's the fox to my deer?"

And then a red flag goes off: *DANGER! This rabbit hole ends in depression! Quick! Jump down a different hole!*

"Yeah, well at least I'm not fat. I'm not too skinny either, like that one lady down the block. And at least I don't wear black socks with the wrong pants, or white socks with black shoes. A brown belt with black pants, for God's sake! You men have a grand total of *two* fashion rules, and you can't even figure *those* out?"

That Voice is on a roll now, and it's starting to feel good. Any topic for criticism will do: "Your music is too loud, you little punk!" or "Your music is too quiet. What are you, a grandma? Learn to live a little!"

"Salt on your watermelon? I better not hear you complaining about the cost of your prescription lisinopril!"

"A pound of sugar in your coffee? You deserve to die of diabetes, stupid!"

There it is, the red flag that snaps me out of the trance: the word *stupid*. When the Inner Critic starts calling names, I know I'm in trouble. Time for an intervention.

A few years ago, in the throes of one of Missy's judgefests, I sat down and made a list of my common judgments. It was quite revealing.

Things I Judge People For:
1. Being too fat
2. Being too skinny
3. Being lazy
4. Being too ambitious

5. Not being informed, or being dumb
6. Thinking they're a genius
7. Having no fashion sense
8. Being controlled by fashion trends
9. Having babies too young
10. Having babies too old
11. Being too religious
12. Not believing in anything
13. Being arrogant
14. Not having enough confidence
15. Sleeping around
16. Being a prude
17. Tacky tattoos
18. Not having tattoos
19. People who think Adele is a good singer (she's a shouter!)
20. People who judge other people for liking Coldplay

The list goes on, but that's quite enough. You get the point. You've probably noticed a pattern. There's no way to escape this Inner Critic's judgy eye roll. She finds a way to trap you with no middle ground. It's quite an impressive tactic, when you think about it.

The other interesting thing is that, when I'm really honest about this list, the level of hypocrisy is astounding. I've judged myself for every single one of these things. Except for having babies. I've never had a baby. But I *would* have had babies too young if I hadn't been such a prude. So I can judge myself for having no babies. Problem solved.

This exercise helps make something very clear: I judge others because they are a mirror for me. Their imperfections are irritating because they remind me of my own. It's so much easier to pretend the problem is over there instead of right here. Judging others becomes the armor I wear to convince myself I'm better than others. It's not a cute habit.

On the flip side, the things I don't like about others can be things I secretly envy. Take being lazy, for example. How many times have I wished I could just learn to relax and allow myself to do nothing, to just *be*? And those ambitious, successful people? I admire them for their courageousness and persistence, but I am too afraid to take those risks myself!

Missy Prissy was really lacking in love for herself. Maybe she had never been given permission to be an equal with others. This poor girl needed some good ol'-fashioned motherly love. I realized I could give her some nurturing whenever she started acting up. For starters, I decided to write her a letter:

Dear Missy,

I love you. I know it's hard to believe because you're trying to mask your imperfections and insecurities so that no one sees your flaws. I know you don't believe—and cannot yet fully embrace—the reality that Love takes delight in our imperfections and completely accepts them!

Do you really feel better about yourself after dissing others? Does the constant judge-parade in your head truly help you feel loved and at peace? Or does it just create more noise followed by desperate attempts to cover and justify your slander?

I know you've been hurt. I know you're terrified of society's impossible standards. And I know self-righteousness gives you a sense of power. Today, I invite you to try a new tactic: Accept yourself. With all your zits and freckles and split ends. With all your messy thoughts, dreams, motivations, strangeness, and emotions. Don't cover it anymore, because the world is missing out on the real, beautiful, vulnerable you!

Godde already knows you are imperfect. She made you that way on purpose so that you'd be interesting, funny, and wise. She loves you unconditionally. No joke. No dirty tricks. Even with a failing grade or a tiny savings account, you are loved! Delighted in! Cherished! You are gorgeous just the way you are. You are valuable because you exist, not because of your looks or accomplishments. So put down your mask; it's such a heavy load.

Try delighting in others. Take joy in their happiness. Love their imperfections. It makes them interesting and funny. It makes them equals; and while disrupting the established hierarchy is threatening, it opens up the possibility of true friendship and intimacy. Being better than everyone is a lonely place to be.

Time to let go. Time to taste freedom. Time to shine your little light, with kindness leading the way. Kindness is the light. I love you.

Your imperfect friend,
Chelsea

YOUR TURN!
Inner Work Exercises

1. Set a Timer for Five Minutes and Write Down All the Things for Which You Judge Yourself

Keep writing until the timer goes off, without censoring your thoughts. When these judgments stay in my mind, they somehow seem reasonable. But on paper, they are ridiculous. They could also be viewed as embarrassing and disheartening. But being disappointed in ourselves doesn't help anyone. Remember, the goal here is to observe ourselves *objectively,* without judgment. Once I see my judgments on paper, I realize I'm really quite sick of them and I don't need them. There is something magical about shifting these criticisms to a visible, external space. Writing them down takes a big portion of their momentum and power away. We begin to admit our secrets to ourselves.

2. Set a Timer for Five Minutes and Write Down All the Things for Which You Judge Other People

They can be general themes, but the more specific you can get, the better. Be brutally honest. No one will see this but you. (Unless you are silly enough to publish a book about it!) Keep writing without stopping until the timer goes off.

3. Read Your Two Lists Out Loud to Yourself

Then set a timer for ten minutes, and do a freewrite in response to your lists. What did you notice? Are there any patterns? Your patterns may be different from mine. Just get curious. Where did you learn these judgments? What feelings are coming up right now? Jot it all down.

4. When the Timer Goes Off, Take a Few More Minutes to Write a Compassionate and Understanding Letter to the Judgy Part of Yourself
This is hard stuff to look at. Acknowledge this. You didn't consciously choose these judgments, and they don't make you a bad person. They are just thoughts.

5. Bring In Some Humor and Forgiveness
Does this part of you have a name? A tone of voice? What age is this part of you? Do any of the judgments seem silly from this perspective? Can you even, perhaps, laugh at them (and yourself) a little? If you discovered another Inner Critic character during this exercise, you may want to sketch this one as well.

CHAPTER 5:
Sister Mary Chastity Constance of the Immaculate Righteousness

*I'm not stayin' in no damn convent with these people.
These people don't even have sex!*
—Deloris, *Sister Act*

There is a section of my bookshelf that is covered up by a piece of my friend's watercolor artwork. The placement is intentional. Even though the book behind it is on a private shelf in my bedroom, where the door is always kept closed, I can't bring myself to let the title show itself openly. Perhaps I am mostly keeping it hidden from myself: *Completely Overcome Vaginismus.* Why would I want the daily reminder that I'm not completely there yet? It is the shadow that looms in the back of my mind: *What if my body and mind are permanently broken and dysfunctional? What if I can never have a normal sex life, one of freedom and pleasure? I'm too old for this shit. What the hell is wrong with me?*

You might not know what this mysterious and clinical-sounding word means. But vaginismus had been the thorn in my flesh, the bane of my existence ever since I hit puberty. It is the involuntary contraction of the pelvic floor muscles that surround the vagina, closing the opening with such vigor that any penetration is painful at best and impossible at worst. The best way to explain it is that my vagina has a panic attack when anything approaches it—and no level of deep breathing, stretching, or foreplay can stop it. It has a mind of its own. It is trauma trapped in my muscles. It is a pattern of fearful thinking that has manifested physically. I only know this now, in hindsight, after working on this through several therapeutic methods, therapies, and research. Medical doctors only added to the trauma. They didn't get it. No one has ever given me the option of a smaller-sized speculum when I go in for routine pap smears, even though I'm clearly panicking, tears streaming down my face, my legs shuddering and snapping closed despite instructions to "just relax."

When I was in high school, the stakes weren't very high, so I could mostly ignore it. All I knew was that all of my friends had started using tampons and, after three years of trying, I still didn't believe that I had a hole down there. I would lock myself in the bathroom, turn on some Enya, do all my tai chi relaxation exercises, and slowly try to insert the tampon. Nothing. Just a wall down there. When I nonchalantly shared that I chose not to use tampons and tried to play it off, my best friend said, "You need to use tampons. You won't be able to have sex otherwise!"

My heart dropped into my abdomen with a thud that echoed down to my toes, but I quickly brushed it off. *Whatever*, I thought. *I'll be fine. I'm not going to have sex until marriage anyway; and when it's with my husband, it will be magical and beautiful.* This belief that my vagina would miraculously be cured as a reward for my faithfulness, that it would suddenly start shooting out puppies and rainbows on my wedding night, was a lie I held on to for longer than I'd like to admit. But who could blame me, after all the church youth group pep talks I'd been through? (*Your sexuality is like a sandwich. If you let everyone have a bite, there will be nothing left for your spouse!*) After all the brainwashing Disney flicks that I'd watched on repeat? (*And they lived happily ever after.*) After being presented with only one misogynistic view of the female body?

Being taught to repress and fear my sexuality came at me from all angles. My fourth-grade teacher was tasked with giving us the reproductive health talk. Instead, she just asked, "So who here does *not* know where babies come from? No one? No one? Okay, good. Moving on."

What! I screamed inside. *They all know but me? Why am I so far behind? Baby-making must be horrible if she doesn't want to talk about it!*

In my teenager years, my father would cover his ears and run from the room if I mentioned the word *period*. (*Okay,* I'd think. *So I'm dirty and gross. Got it.*) My mom would insist that my skirts go to my knees and that my collarbone not show on any of the clothes she made me. (*My body is something to be covered up. If I don't, I lead myself into danger—or lead men into sin. Check!*) Ninth-grade sex ed consisted of a graphic slideshow of genitals covered in STDs, a lecture on how abstinence is the only way, and my teacher's explanation that girls don't need to masturbate because they don't have that need for sexual release like boys do. (*Sex is for men, not women.*)

One of my best friends told me about her first pap smear when we were sixteen. "It was the most painful thing I've ever experienced!" she exclaimed, tears brimming in her eyes. (*Okay, so just avoid penetration at all costs. Easy. That was my plan anyway.*) My worrywart father, with every good intention, didn't want me to leave the house without pepper spray. "Don't rollerblade alone!" he'd warn. "There are rapists down by that river trail!" (*All men are potential rapists. Good to know.*) I prayed, along with thousands of fans at a Rebecca St. James concert, to be given the courage and faithfulness to save myself for marriage, committing myself to Jesus alone. (*God hates fornicators. Hell awaits them.*)

I could go on, but you get the picture. Now you're starting to see why almost anything could be a potential slippery slope toward sexual deviancy. My body and my sexuality were the things to be feared, above all else.

When I left home to go to Wartburg College, a surprisingly progressive liberal arts school in the middle of the corn fields of Iowa, I began to accumulate different perspectives on bodies, sex, and relationships. Throughout college, I slowly accepted that my lady bits were flawed after listening to other female friends talk about tampons, sex, and masturbation. I just listened and never shared my freakishness. I let them assume I was sexually active and loving it, just like everyone else claimed to be.

However, I was resourceful. I finally worked up the courage at age twenty-three to ask my roommate how to give a blow job. "Girl, I'm taking you to Barnes & Noble!" she said, laughing. We hopped on the bus to the store in downtown Minneapolis, and she directed me to the section with a shelf full of sex advice (the Internet was barely a thing back then). Turns out there are lots of ways to have sex without penetration (hallelujah!), and I was ready to master them all. I bought a book full of illustrations, detailed instructions, and testimonials. I read that four-hundred-page document from cover to cover within days.

As they say, knowledge is power, and I set out on my quest with a confidence I had never known. The first guy I came across was easy. He would take whatever he could get, and he wasn't pushy. We were having casual fun, but I was starting to really like him. Then I found out through a little birdie that he was actually cheating on his girlfriend with me. Ouch. (*You idiot, Chelsea! Shake it off. On to the next guy.*) After a few make-out sessions, I decided it was important to tell him that I was a virgin. He dismissed me with one sentence: "Yo, you're way too old for that." He wanted nothing else to do with me.

My mind short-circuited then: *I thought virginity in women was desirable! Have I been doing my whole life wrong? Did I miss the prime window of acceptable deflowering somewhere between ages nineteen to twenty-one? I'm hopeless! Pitiable! Completely fucked! (No, that's the wrong term, nitwit! Your pathetic, malfunctioning pussy has completely unfucked you. You're going to die sad and alone, an eighty-nine-year-old virgin! You might as well join the convent now, because ain't nobody gonna want you but God!)*

Enter Sister Mary Chastity Constance of the Immaculate Righteousness. She has been with me for about twenty years, and her voice is filled with shaming tirades, self-blame, pity parties, and victim-playing as a way to opt out of taking further risks. Over the years, she has tried (oftentimes successfully) to convince me that I am an inept, eternal child who doesn't have the capacity to grow up, especially when it comes to anything remotely related to sex. She can get on my case over any number of things: my sexuality, my body, being single, shaming me for being attracted to addicts, pointing out areas where I've tried and failed. She loves to remind me that I'm trapped, broken, gross, and alone.

SISTER MARY CHASTITY CONSTANCE

Sometimes she branches out on to other topics. For example, after the third job interview in a row with no follow-up offer, she started yapping, "See? I *told* you that it's not worth trying anything other than this godforsaken convent! You've got nothing to offer that the world wants. Just face it. You already hit your peak with that worthless barista job. Just take her now, Jesus, 'cause you really made a mistake on *this* creation!"

So who is this tyrannical nun? Her image and story came to me instantly one day out of the blue. She is a sister who has spent her lifetime trying to follow the rules and do the right thing, but she's pissed about it. The resentment seethes out of every pore of her body. (*How come I'm stuck here, playing by the rules and locked away in this shit hole, while all y'all get to run around, doing whatever the hell you want? Why am I the only one who cares, who has to be the good girl, the perpetual servant, the societal reformer? Go ahead and have your frivolous fun, you irresponsible schmucks! I'm the one holding it down for all of us. The world would fall apart if it weren't for me!*) Every once in a while, she sneaks out and smokes her cigarettes and drinks her forbidden liquor out on the back steps of the nunnery when no one else is looking. It sounds like she's ragging on others, but most of her energy is channeled self-loathing. She is *resentful*.

Around age twenty-six, I found myself in a clinic, attempting to have the recommended pap smear exam. While I had been to a few other doctors for this checkup (with embarrassing panic attacks and extreme pain), this was the first practitioner to tell me there was a name for my condition. She casually handed me a printout on vaginismus and said, "Don't worry. It's curable." When I got home, I instantly read the packet. *Check, check, check.* All the symptoms and descriptions fit. *Oh my God, I'm not a freak! There are other people like me!* With growing excitement, I began to search the Internet. There wasn't much there, but I found a vaginismus workbook to order, along with some mysterious thing called a vaginal dilator. Turns out this is a set of oblong silicone objects of various sizes that are inserted into the vagina to practice relaxing the pelvic floor muscles. The smallest is the size of my pinky finger, the next about the size of my thumb, all the way up to the size of a large banana.

SISTER MARY CHASTITY CONSTANCE

When they arrived in the mail, I committed fully to the suggestions in the book, reading the information and testimonials, working through the journaling exercises, practicing daily Kegel (pelvic floor) exercises, and—after about three months—practicing daily dilator insertion. The journaling helped deconstruct my twisted, shame-ridden views about sex and bodies. I also talked, cried, and prayed with my spiritual director about the subject for years; and I saw a few different types of therapists about my affliction. Eight years later, I *still* couldn't have pain-free sex like a "normal" woman, not without the awkward help of dilators in the bedroom. "Excuse me," I'd say. "I know you're rarin' to go, but can you just hold that thought for five minutes while I work my way up to the dilator that correlates with the size of your penis?" I felt hopeless, ashamed, and broken. After all this work, I had a greater understanding of my condition, but not much else to show for it. Sister Mary was in her heyday, enjoying each of my failures as an opportunity to gloat.

One day, at my favorite café, someone had drawn a little picture of a cactus with a face on the chalkboard menu and labeled it "Caleb the Cactus." It had been there for months. I used to love that little cactus. Back when I had a huge crush on a boy named Caleb, I took a picture of it and texted it to him. I don't think he ever responded, per usual. Somehow I always end up chasing dudes who don't chase me back. It's a lopsided effort, every time.

Now, whenever I see that little cactus, I sigh and feel myself doing an internal eye roll. *Damn that cactus. I'm sick of sitting at this table alone. Drinking this Americano alone. Going to movies alone. Going to the beach and the park alone. Out to eat alone. Bike rides alone. Dying under a bridge alone.* Well, I haven't actually done that last one, but I've imagined that scenario too many times. It's narrated in an old woman's voice, scratchy and rough from a lifetime of smoking cigarettes. She lets me know that it's my fault that I'm alone: *Your stupid ass brought this upon yourself, you know. And you have the nerve to think you'll ever find someone who reciprocates your love? Keep dreaming, dumbass! No such person exists—not for you anyway.*

Fuck you, Sister Mary Chastity! You don't run me! A knot forms in my stomach, and my body slowly dissolves. I'm no longer here. All that exists is a mind that is frantically running through my list of contacts, searching for a potential mate—anyone. Even ex-partners begin to look appealing. I forget the reasons I broke up with them: alcoholism, misogyny, homelessness. (*I'm sure they've changed by now. What would one little text hurt, just to say "hi"? I've got to prove that cruel nun wrong. You're just a voice in my head, not the truth! Shut up!*)

Acquiesce, Rebel, Justify

When the Inner Critic strikes, there are a few common reactions that most of us jump to internally. (At least I do.) The first option is to acquiesce to its tyranny, rolling over and accepting it as truth. Sometimes the voice is so subtle and alluring that I don't even notice when it is operating. In these circumstances, it seeps into my consciousness and begins to eat away at my sense of self-worth. (*I'm useless, a hopeless nobody. Why bother trying?*) The resulting feeling can be depression, numbness, or lethargy. Or perhaps I lash out at others in anger. Procrastination and inaction kick in as a response to these beliefs. The Inner Critic has won. It has convinced me I am unworthy.

If complying with the Inner Critic doesn't work, then perhaps rebelling against it will. When it rears its ugly head, I will rear mine. Fists up—don't let it get to you. When it starts slinging insults and lies, I'll rebel against it. (*Fuck you, Inner Critic! You're not the boss of me! Just watch. I'll prove you wrong!*) To rebel against the Inner Critic, I feel a desperate need for tangible proof that it's wrong. So I go out and do something stupid, like text an old boyfriend, buy a padded bra and mascara that my low-maintenance self will never wear, or befriend someone I don't actually like just to prove I'm a nice person. Then the Inner Critic has one more reason to rip me apart for being impulsive, shallow, insecure, or needy. Again, the Inner Critic has won.

Okay, so neither being submissive to the Inner Critic nor fighting against it works. Perhaps logic can win the day. If I can identify it as just a thought pattern, I can remember not to believe everything I think. Thoughts and feelings aren't facts, so I'll prove it by stating logical counterpoints, tried-and-true philosophies, and real-life examples to prove that *I'm* right, not the cruel voice in my head. The problem here is that the Inner Critic has a way of slipping right past logic and pushing all my emotional triggers. It knows me too well. As I argue with it, it argues back, gaining momentum and energy. My irritation grows as the arguments repeat themselves, circling around and around in a vortex of desperation. Once the centrifugal force starts spinning, it's hard to jump off the merry-go-round. The inertia is powerful because the axis it's revolving around is the belief that I need to justify myself to a Demon whose only job is to criticize, which is a losing battle. The Demon will always have the last word.

So where is the hope? The problem with all of the above strategies is that they *engage* the Inner Critic from the assumption that it might hold the truth, which gives it more fuel. To acquiesce, rebel against, or justify myself to the Inner Demons will never work, because each of these reactions is trying to fix the mind with the mind. When the mind is caught up in reactivity, the body and the heart feel a million miles away. And yet it is the heart and the body that will pull us out of this mess. What we need is a *measured, intentional response* instead of a knee-jerk reaction. We need to get out of our heads and back into reality.

Metta

Let's go back to New Year's Eve 2012. I had been invited by a friend to go to a meditation center to hear her favorite local singer-songwriter perform. As I walked through the doors, something deep within me perked up. Everyone here was either smiling and talking softly or sitting cross-legged in silence, eyes closed, hands resting gently in their laps. Not your typical New Year's bash. No blaring music, no decorations. Just a comforting stillness, the empty beige walls beautifully accentuated by a small shelf with a wooden Buddha statue and a vase with two strategically placed live flowers. The lights were dim, soothing my spirit into a place of openness and curiosity. *What is this place?* I asked myself.

My friend and I had unknowingly arrived an hour early, and we were told the loving-kindness meditation was about to begin. We were very welcome, and we were invited to join in. I didn't really know what "loving-kindness meditation" meant. But it sounded pleasant, so we stayed.

As I settled onto my cushion on the floor, my body was alert yet relaxed—a combination with which I was not yet familiar. The lights dimmed further, and I closed my eyes. The teacher up front began to guide us, gently telling us where to place our attention, starting with sounds, then bodily sensations, then the breath. We were then directed to bring to mind some being we easily loved, someone with whom we had an uncomplicated relationship. A pet or a small child would be best. I chose one of my favorite students from the after-school program I used to work at, a five-year-old child I had often wished I could adopt. As I continued to picture this child playing and laughing, I was instructed to notice the feelings that arose within my body and to begin wishing this being happiness, safety, protection, and peace.

To my amazement, I could actually feel my chest expanding. It felt like my heart was going to explode in the best way possible, a sweet pain that kept growing. I could no longer tell if my heart was still contained within my body. Its borders seemed to encompass everyone in this room. We were told that the Pali word for this feeling was *metta*.

"Focus on the feeling of love and kindness," the teacher went on to say. "Notice if anything gets in the way, then go back to the feeling of metta. Now, bring to mind a neutral person in your life who you don't really know. Perhaps the cashier at your local grocery store, or the neighbor at the end of the block. Now, allow the feeling of loving-kindness to be directed toward this person. Just like me, they are a person with difficulties, suffering, and dreams. May they also be happy, safe, protected, and at peace."

My whole body was feeling light then, lifting upward. Although my leg was beginning to fall asleep, I didn't care. My attention was on the ocean of love I had discovered within me.

After staying with the neutral person for several minutes, we moved on to a difficult person, someone with whom we had some conflict or irritation. My breathing was slow and deep, and I remember easily transferring the love that had started with my beloved student to this annoying person who had come to mind. They, too, were worthy of love and acceptance, because their lives were also difficult, and they had needs and pain, just like I did.

We moved on to sending loving-kindness to everyone in the room, everyone in our city, then the state, the country, and the world. We even sent good intentions out into the cosmos. For once in my life, my mind was blank. I was only a heart, pulsing with care. The energy of the 120 other people in the room, sending out their blessings, was palpable. My good intentions were being carried by theirs.

And then, the kicker. "Now, bring the love and care back, right here, and direct it toward yourself, toward your own heart," the teacher said. "Place your hand on your chest, if that helps. Send yourself well wishes, acknowledging that it is hard to be a human being with a life, with a body, with feelings, with a conditioned mind. Send yourself phrases of love. May you be happy. May you be safe and protected, healthy and strong. May you be a friend to your body and live at ease. May you experience contentedness and peace."

What! I thought. *Love myself? You mean to tell me that is an option?* At first, it felt wrong. Selfish. Conceited. But the momentum of the metta was so strong that it overpowered my years of conditioning. The wisdom within me knew that this was right and good. Without cognition, I suddenly understood what Jesus meant when he said, "You shall love your neighbor as you love yourself." It was less of a commandment and more of a statement about the nature of things, about the cause and effect of karma. He could also have said, "As you hate your neighbor, so shall you hate yourself." When we don't love ourselves, we have no solid ground to stand on from which to offer love to others. But when we love ourselves, neuroses and all, our heart loosens enough to stop comparing ourselves to others, judging others, and turning others into enemies. The extent to which I offer love to myself *is* the extent to which I offer love to others. "You *shall* love your neighbor as you love yourself." Period.

In the last moments of the guided meditation, I noticed tears were beginning to dry on my cheeks. My whole life, I had been trying so hard to do the right thing, striving to be a loving person, getting twisted up in knots because it was never enough. And I was a loving person. But this was the first time I had allowed my heart to fully feel and be open to the love that had been hiding right under the surface the whole time. A deep well of compassion was right here within me, and I had finally been given the bucket to draw from its sweet source.

Herein lies the antidote to the inner torment of the Inner Critic. It is an intentional move from the head down into the heart, calling on compassion, remembering that it is hard to be a human being, that it is hard to have an Inner Critic (or a whole jury of them!). What metta meditation taught me was that love can be cultivated. It's not something some people are born with more of and others have less of. Just like growing a seed in a garden takes the right elements and conditions, we can provide the conditions to grow loving-kindness toward ourselves and others. When the Inner Critic rises, simply willing loving thoughts doesn't work. Commanding myself—"Be a loving person! C'mon, Chelsea, love yourself!"—will never work. Wishing away the hatred and shame gets us nowhere unless we choose to consciously *replace* it with something else. What works is stopping, putting a hand on my heart, and saying to myself, "This is really hard right now. Your critic is acting up, and that is painful. May you be happy. May you be safe from self-judgment. May you believe in your worthiness and be at peace."

It turns out Love really is the most tenacious force in the universe. It is not wimpy or soft. It is bold, radical, and transformative. It sweeps in and conquers dragons. Even a whole Legion of Demons has no weaponry strong enough to fight back against Love. And unlike the force of anger, Love leaves no ugly or regretful reverberations in the heart after the battle. It leaves nothing that the Critic can hold against you.

I needed to tell Sister Mary what I had discovered, so I wrote her this letter:

Dearest Sister Mary Chastity,

You've had a hard life. You've been through some really difficult things, so I can see why you're angry at God and afraid to wish for a better future. Resentment feels safer than hope. Optimism and a happy disposition seem threatening to you,

SISTER MARY CHASTITY CONSTANCE

because what if your dreams get dashed? Best to plan for the worst so as not to be disappointed.

But that's a difficult way to live, and it is only one of many options. I know it's hard to believe, but Godde isn't trying to trick or trap you. I don't blame you for thinking so though, since you were fed so many images of a wrathful, vindictive, distant Terrorist in the Sky. Contrary to these stories, I have come to realize that Godde wants what is best for you; and part of that vision is for you to have a happy life, full of gratitude for all the beauty around you! Each day, your basic needs are met, and you are surrounded by a loving community of friends. They don't see you as a failure for being single, choosing a life of service to Godde, or longing for more. You are human. On the top of our list of basic human needs are love and touch. Of course, you want these things! So please stop projecting your insecurities on to others and playing the martyr.

The timing of the Universe is perfect. Just because you don't have the things you want doesn't mean Godde is torturing you. All it means is that it has not happened yet. Or it could mean that there is an even better path waiting for you than you've imagined. Even in your old age, you have choices. If this convent is a prison to you, leave! Godde will applaud your freedom! Something better is on the horizon, better than following rules, vows, and parental expectations. Instead, follow your heart's deepest desire! Choose joy and gratitude! Choose to trust that Godde can transform your negative thinking, in Godde's time.

Come with me. Let's break out of this prison of negative thoughts! With deep compassion for the struggle and gratitude for your service, I grant you permission to release *your resentments. No more chaste and repressed bodies. Let us now chasten our hearts by purifying them of hate.*

Your Sister in service and love,
Chelsea

PS: Pssst! Hey, Sister! I just put Holy Water inside my vagina to bless it. Thought you'd get a kick out of that. (I know Jesus did.) Give it a try yourself!

YOUR TURN!
Inner Work Exercise

Try a Loving-Kindness Meditation: Chances are it won't be as instantly powerful to you if you aren't sitting in a room with 120 other people doing the same thing. But this practice is transformative over time. Stick with it. Give it a few tries, even if you aren't feeling anything. (You can also find guided loving-kindness meditations online or on meditation apps.)

1. Start by finding a quiet place to sit where you won't be disturbed. It doesn't matter how you sit. Just find a position that is comfortable yet upright.

2. Begin by taking a few deep breaths. Notice how your body is feeling, and loosen any areas of tension.

3. Bring to mind someone who is very easy to love. A small child or an animal is easiest. Picture them happy. Begin reciting these phrases silently to yourself:

> May you be happy.
> May you be safe and protected.
> May you be healthy and strong.
> May you be peaceful and at ease.

If these exact phrases don't work for you, make up your own. When things get really hard, I like to add phrases like these:

May you be a friend to your body.
May you show up for yourself with Love and Wisdom.
I care enough about your suffering to get close.

4. Let your focus of attention be the feeling of loving-kindness that begins to develop within you. Notice the sensations in the body when this feeling is present. Throughout the meditation, when distracting or doubtful thoughts come up, gently make a note of them and return to your intention of cultivating metta in your heart.

5. Move through the following progression of people, and send each one your loving-kindness and recite the phrases of concern:

   a. Benefactor: A person who has added love and value to your life.

   b. Neutral Person: Someone you see often but don't know personally.

   c. Difficult Person: Don't pick the most difficult person you know. That tends to be too difficult and interrupts the flow of metta. Just pick someone who has been annoying you lately.

   d. Yourself: Remember that you also deserve to be included in the circle of love and care!

   e. The Whole World: Include all beings—people, animals, insects, plants—since they all want to be happy and healthy!

6. When you're ready, take a few more conscious breaths and slowly open your eyes. Carry this sense of loving-kindness into all of your interactions today. Everyone is deserving of love. Above all, send gentle care to yourself today, because it's hard being a human.

CHAPTER 6:
The Imposter Police

The sinner is actually one who does not love himself enough.
—St. Teresa of Ávila

So far, all the Inner Critics I've presented have been highly critical and angry. Perhaps you resonate with these cruel voices. But maybe you are also thinking, *Geez, she's so pissed all the time! I can't relate to that at all. Thank goodness! It must mean I don't have an Inner Critic.* Think again. There are many different versions and flavors of the Inner Critic, and some are sneakier than others. Some seem downright intelligent, helpful, and protective. Enter the Imposter Police.

It was our first day of class for spiritual direction training. I had been accepted into a two-year certification program that provided formative instruction, supervision, and internship for aspiring spiritual directors. As I walked into the room, my heart sank. Everyone there was *at least* two decades older than me. A few had more than four decades more of life experience than me. There was a minimum age limit to apply to this program, and I had barely squeezed in at age thirty. *Shit!* I thought. *Perhaps if I keep my mouth shut the whole time, no one will notice that I don't belong here and that I don't know what the heck I'm doing with my life. They'll just assume I'm amazing and wise. What if they find out I'm all questions and no answers? I'll be kicked out for sure!*

As the instructor began the orientation, I realized my initial strategy of silence wouldn't be an option. This was a participatory program. Interactive, with small-group sharing and large-group sharing.

You're in over your head this time, kid, an enthusiastic Inner Voice chimed in. *I tried to warn you that you need more life experience. You're too young to be placing yourself in the "wise person" chair. And you don't even have all your inner shit straightened out yet. You're a hot mess! I told you to just stick with the conventional job. You've already got a degree in social work, and those jobs are stable. There's no shortage of people who need case managers—and great job security! What's that? You felt like gouging your eyes out with a spoon when you tried being a social worker? So what?! That's because you only got a bachelor's degree. Quit this hocus-pocus spiritual direction nonsense that no one knows about, and go back to grad school. With a master's in social work, life will be easy-breezy! Conventional! Guaranteed income! I'm tellin' ya, kid, this woo-woo program is gonna ruin your life. Quit now before it's too late!*

And so the seed of doubt was planted. Maybe that feeling of doubt was on to something. I barely even knew what this program entailed. I had made this decision based on a feeling in my gut and a recommendation from a trusted mentor. I was taking a huge risk here. And it was true, there hadn't been much logic involved in my decision-making. Once I finished this program, how would I find clients? I wasn't a business-minded person. How would I market myself? No one even knew what spiritual direction was. How do you tell people they need something they aren't even aware exists?

" . . . your name, your religious or spiritual background, and a little bit about why you decided to enroll in this program."

Oh, right. The instructor has been talking. Focus, Chelsea!

Yikes. The big reveal that I was a phony was coming right up. Did I really need to introduce my little millennial ass in front of all these wise sages? I could feel my face turning red. *Please, Godde, don't let me cry in front of them.*

As the introductions began, I perked up. Everyone else in the room seemed as mystified by this process as I was. Some were there to simply learn to be better listeners, or to deepen their own spiritual life that they had largely neglected while raising a family and focusing on a career. Some wanted these skills to complement the work they were already doing. And some admitted they had no idea why they were there! What a relief.

THE IMPOSTER POLICE

As the sharing continued, I realized that several of them had only been meeting with a spiritual director for a couple of years or had just started to do so, since that was a required piece of participating in the training. It slowly dawned on me that, in some ways, I was the most qualified person in the room. I had been meeting with my spiritual director for eight consecutive years by that point, as well as doing deep inner work through the Twelve Step program.

When it was my turn, I took a deep breath and tapped into my Inner Wisdom. Then I reminded myself silently, *There is a reason why I'm here, even if I don't understand yet. I am called to this work, even if I don't know how it will play out logistically. Right now, my only job is to be present to these people, to this process, and take it one class at a time.*

This seems like a good time to take a little tangent and explain more about what spiritual direction is and how I stumbled upon it. To do so, I have to rewind the story to 2007. I was fresh out of college and working my first adult job as an after-school arts coordinator at a little nonprofit in north Minneapolis. (Take that, misguided dermatologist! Your career advice was shabby! One *could* make a living as an artist after all!) I was also attending this amazing interracial church that focused on the liberation of the oppressed, the joys and strengths of community, and loving Godde and loving people, pure and simple.

As part of this church, I started attending monthly social gatherings for young adults, mostly people in their twenties. Strangely, there was always this woman in her sixties who would show up and hang out with us. Her name was Janet. I guess she was the only one who took it literally when we announced, "This group is for the young and the young at heart. All are welcome!"

For one of our monthly gatherings, Janet offered to host us at her apartment, where she would lead a discussion on spirituality and sexuality. I had never heard those two words together in a sentence: spirituality *and* sexuality. I was terrified, but I knew I needed to go, if not to just listen. By this point, I had gathered that I was still highly sheltered, ignorant, closed-minded, and repressed in matters relating to sexual expression; and that part of me was screaming to be liberated. I decided to go, even though I was worried God might strike me down for indulging in impure conversation. Curiosity got the best of me. Janet seemed like a deeply spiritual and happy person, so if she said we could talk about sex at church, I was going to, dammit!

Honestly, I don't remember much about the detailed content of that group discussion. I recall many people sharing (somewhat casually) about premarital sex, love, and even affairs. But what was even more interesting was Janet's response to each person's sharing. She was open, calm, and curious; and she asked follow-up questions that had no hint of shame or blame. What was happening?

I was too terrified to share anything in the group, but afterward I went up to Janet and asked if we could talk one-on-one sometime. She wholeheartedly accepted. Something in me was awakened during that conversation, something that I knew needed attention and healing. I began to understand that, just maybe, my sexuality wasn't evil, dirty, or something to be contained. It was something inherently good—even sacred, perhaps. At least I could hope.

I began to meet with Janet to talk through my upbringing, my oppressive and judging images of God, and the culture of purity in which I had been raised. I told her how I'd learned that not only was my sexuality sinful, but also that having a female body was in itself a thing of shame. I cried (a lot). She listened. I ranted and aired my resentments and regrets. She accepted me. And always, she gently brought me back around to Love. She gave me permission to be a human, to fire my old God and hire a new one; and she instilled in me a sense of true faith in the unfolding process of my life. Over several years of listening sessions like this, I became a new person. I learned to forgive myself and others. I learned to express my feelings in a vulnerable way without shame and fear. I learned that my anger didn't make me a bad person. When I was with Janet, I was reminded that Godde was with me and loved me *just as I am*. Over those years, the intellectual belief that "God loves me" started to sink into my bones.

After about six years of meeting like this, Janet finally shared with me that she was a spiritual director. "Is that what we've been doing this whole time?" I asked. "What is a spiritual director, exactly?"

Janet explained to me that a spiritual director is a "soul friend" who accompanies a person through the path of spiritual discovery, joy and pain, questions and doubts. It's a loving, nonjudgmental process that allows a person to acknowledge their wounds and enter a space of healing. The core work of spiritual direction supports people in deepening their trust in a loving God, Goodness, or Goddess, and in listening and noticing where Spirit is leading and showing up. Spiritual direction is different from counseling in that there is no specific end goal to accomplish, other than continued spiritual freedom and a deepening sense of loving relationships with oneself, others, and God. I discovered that all parts of life are suitable topics for spiritual direction, since the things that affect our hearts, minds, and bodies inevitably affect the Essence of our being (i.e., our spirits and/or souls).

The practice of spiritual direction began to remind me of peeling an onion. As we explore our questions, we also take time to rest in the unquenchable love of God (or the Universe, our Higher Power, Spirit, Source, etc.). It is this Love, and our willingness to let it in, that heals our wounds. As we heal, we grow in self-confidence and gain the courage to approach the next layer, to go a bit deeper. I have found that as soon as one area of our Being is healed, the next layer of work will present itself. Luckily, the practice of spiritual direction allows each person to move at their own pace, as doing deep inner work can be tiring, frightening, and painful. But much more frequently, it is found to be life-giving, joyful, and liberating. Layer by layer, we discover our True Selves by letting go of unnecessary and limiting ideas and attitudes. Along the way, we catch glimpses of and move closer to what lies at our core: Boundless Love and Peace.

Talking with Janet about spiritual direction lit me up. A bright bell of awareness was ringing in the back of my mind. This was the thing I felt I had been searching for all my life! After discovering I didn't enjoy being a social worker, I'd thought long and hard about becoming a pastor or therapist, but neither of those ever felt quite right. To my delight, Janet suggested I look into some certification programs for spiritual direction because she thought I would be good at it. Thus it was that I ended up in that room with a bunch of retirees, with self-doubt creeping in, making me think, *I'm too young for this. Quit now, before they discover you're a phony!*

Imposter syndrome is a term that has become commonplace these days. Most of us know what it means, and most of us have experienced it in some form or another. It is a sinking feeling that we are somehow inadequate for the task ahead of us, whether that be a new job, a new relationship, or a decision to learn a new hobby. Imposter syndrome has a flavor of anxiety to it, as well as a feeling of self-doubt. We suddenly question our decisions and capabilities, compare ourselves to others, and think someone else could fulfill this role better than us (and, we think, perhaps they should). It usually comes with the belief that you don't deserve success, or that the success you are currently enjoying is somehow not legitimate. (*If they ever find out who I really am, they'll fire me for sure!*)

When I thought about this Inner Critic character, a police officer instantly came to mind. The officer begins investigating my credentials and wants to see an ID. She reassures me that she's there to serve and protect me, giving me constant warnings about how I'm speeding too fast into situations that could embarrass me, ruin my reputation, or—worst of all—lead to *failure*.

The most important thing to note about the Imposter Police is that they show up whenever we decide to take a risk or move outside of our comfort zone into a new experience. If the Imposter Police had it their way, we would just stay in that dead-end job or with that deadbeat partner until our dying days. At least we would know what to expect. There would be no surprises, no challenges. Sure, life would become monotonous, but the Imposter Police prefer that over any sort of risk. They want a sure path, with no surprises.

These inner officers who convince us to stay comfortable love to remind us that it's not *smart* to put our necks on the line. They assure us that we will be humiliated if we follow our dreams. They are well-intentioned, trying to keep us from getting hurt or ending up broke. At times, there can be some trustworthy guidance here. It *is* smart to do our homework before making big decisions or get some training before we start a new business. But the Imposter Police like to lay out all the steps that would be necessary to achieve our dream, remind us how difficult each step would be and how failure is likely, and then convince us to drop the whole thing.

When logic is not enough to turn us away from our heart's desire, the Imposter Police will turn to shaming tactics: *Who do you think you are? You don't deserve this. Other people are much more qualified than you. Go back where you belong!*

The absurd thing about the "logic" behind imposter syndrome is that it doesn't take into account that *every single person* who is living their dream started from a place of knowing nothing. Every dream is built one step at a time. By reading books, training, and practicing. By trying and failing. By learning from each mistake. By trying again. By receiving mentorship. And *every step is manageable*, when we break it down into small pieces. The Imposter Police would have us believe that we need to figure it all out right now, every detail of every step of the path. But life doesn't work that way. All we can ever do is the next right thing.

After three years of working at the after-school program in north Minneapolis, I began talking to my boss, Mary Lou, about whether I should move to Mexico. I had a job offer at a school down there that I was really excited about. I was in an anxious place, trying to figure out all the possible outcomes of my moving there. Would I stay at that job after my year-long contract ended? What if my Spanish wasn't good enough? Could I move to another place in Mexico and find different work? Would I stay in Mexico and never return to the States? Every scenario sounded risky. At one point, I was thinking, *Maybe I should just stay here in Minneapolis in this entry-level job for the rest of my life, supervising kids while they paint on walls. At least I'd know what to expect.* I had no idea what I was getting myself into if I moved to Mexico.

Then Mary Lou told me something I'll never forget. She said, "Sometimes we wish we could just see our whole future laid out before us, how everything is going to work out. But if we saw that, we would be terrified by our greatness, and we would be too scared to even begin the journey. So instead, we are given these mysterious little internal nudges—flashes of desire that point us to the next right step. When we work up the courage to take that step, only from that new vantage point can we see clearly what the *next* step will be. This is just the

way life is. It requires faith. Faith in yourself and your capabilities, and faith that you will never be left alone without guidance on any step of this journey."

So I moved to Mexico. It didn't turn out the way I'd planned, not in the least. It was actually kind of a disaster. But it did launch me into the next chapter of my life in a way that was far better than anything I could have planned on my own. What I learned from this was that those mysterious inner "nudges" are there for a reason, even if we can't initially figure out why. The nudge to quit that job, to move across the country, to ask that person out, to go back to school or take a course, to read a certain book or pick up a new hobby—they all lead us to the next good thing. It is not our job to make sense of intuition. It is our job to *listen*.

And we have a choice. We can listen to our Inner Guidance or the Imposter Police. Which one has our best interests in mind? It can seem like the self-doubt is here to protect us—and in a way, it is! It is just misguided in its methods. It thinks that *any* discomfort or fear is a sign of imminent danger, when in fact a nervous stomach might be the excitement of finally following your heart's desire! The nerves and lack of appetite before a big job interview will be interpreted the same as a tiger chasing you. There is no tiger awaiting you in that interview. There is only the possibility of you spreading your wings out to their full breadth so that you can finally feel what it's like to fly.

I recently had a strong attack of Imposter Syndrome. It plagued me for several months on end because I was steadily moving toward a choice that it perceived as downright foolish. I was going to quit my job that provided a full benefits package and move into self-employment full time. *This will be a disaster!* the Imposter Police said. *You know nothing about marketing, taxes, bookkeeping, or maintaining a client base. You're certain to end up homeless under a bridge this time!*

For the past three years, I had been slowly building my side business, offering spiritual direction and Enneagram education while working as a teacher's assistant at a public school. I hated the school job. It was torture. Sure, it had its good moments (the kids were cute and hilarious), but mostly it consisted of managing one traumatic moment after another and my nervous system was shot. I was constantly hyperalert, scanning the room or the schoolyard for the next fight to break out so that I could run over and break it up. Or anticipating the next "jail break," with some kid running away across the busy street. Or the sneaky, insidious bullying and gossip that gets passed through "he said, she said" and name calling. Children can be vicious.

Meanwhile, my business was growing. I was gaining confidence in my skills and collecting a following of people who resonated with the courses and workshops I offered. I knew I had a lot to offer, and I wanted to ditch the school job so that I could dedicate 100 percent of my energy to what I knew was my clear calling. I even wrote out a mission statement: "Encouraging and holding space for the opening of hearts, minds, bodies, and souls to healing and wholeness, that we might move toward Peace."

But I wasn't yet making enough money to quit my job and sustain myself. On the other hand, how could I ever make enough money through my business when the school job was draining all my time and energy? Besides, living in one's Purpose isn't all about money! Still, I felt stuck—and the Imposter Police had plenty of opinions about my dilemma: *The school job makes logistical sense. It's only thirty hours a week, with good pay and good benefits. And it's only five blocks from your house, which saves you time to do all your cute little "spiritual projects" on the side! What more could you ask for? It's perfect!*

"But I hate my job. I'm experiencing vicarious trauma thirty hours a week!"

What's a little PTSD compared to the torture of figuring out self-employment taxes and insurance? You know nothing about that! You hate those things. It's too much of a hassle. Besides, everyone has PTSD. It's no big deal. And plenty of people have it way worse than you.

"But I know this is my calling! I finally found what I'm here on this planet to do! Whenever I'm with a client and offering spiritual direction or Enneagram coaching, I'm in the Flow. I'm completely present, using my gifts to change people's lives in a way that feels nourishing to them *and* me!"

Just settle for living your calling part-time. That's more than most people ever get to do! Don't be so selfish, thinking you deserve to do what you love all week long. If you expect that to happen, you'll just be disappointed when it doesn't work out and you have to go back to work as a barista again.

And on and on it would go.

By some Grace, I was connected with an Enneagram teacher who volunteered to mentor me in starting a self-sustaining business. She offered this freely, even though she was a professional coach. Over several months, we not only talked about the strategy of creating my business plan, but continuously checked in with the state of my fears and doubts about whether I could pull this off. "Trust me," she would say. "If I can do this, anyone can."

"But it feels like jumping off a cliff, not knowing if something will catch me or if I'll fall to my death," I told her once.

After a pause, she said, "If you weren't scared to do this, I'd be worried. That just means you're sane. The nervousness also means you're following your heart, which is always terrifying. But once we jump off that cliff, we realize it's just an abyss. There is no bottom, and we can actually learn to trust the free fall. You can trust it because if you're making this leap not only for yourself but also for the benefit of others, the Ground of Being will be there to support you. But first, you gotta jump."

Months passed, and I spent the summer getting things in line for a new ten-month Enneagram course I was offering. If enough people signed up, I could quit my job.

But the BENEFITS PACKAGE! the Imposter Police would remind me.

"We'll just wait and see," I'd say. "And pray." Once the registrations began rolling in, I responded with, "Wow, this might work after all! But I could still work at the school job, just in case."

As the summer came to a close, I was forced into a decision. Then the emails started rolling in about our first staff meeting and enrolling in professional development sessions. I felt sick to my stomach, like I might throw up. My body was screaming at me to quit. The inner war between my intuition and the Imposter Police was raging at full tilt. Eventually, I checked my bank account statement to gather more information. *Wait, what?* I thought. *There's enough money here to sustain me for a whole year, even if I don't make a single dollar through this Enneagram class! What the hell am I waiting for?* The nauseous feeling suddenly turned into electric pulses flowing through my body. I could actually do this. *I am going to do this!*

All of the months (and years!) of encouragement from mentors and friends propelled me as I logged into my work email account and wrote a brief letter of resignation to my boss. My whole body was vibrating with energy, and I was sweating buckets. I took a few deep breaths and silently offered a one-line prayer: *For the benefit of all beings.* Then I hit Send.

The Imposter Police would have us believe otherwise, but the only way to gain competence and confidence in a certain skill is by actually *doing* it. Practice is what makes progress, what builds our knowledge base and credibility. And guess what? Practicing in your head doesn't count. That's not practicing; that's fantasizing and worrying. Sure, there is some benefit to visualization. But it's in the actual *doing* that we learn, and mostly from making mistakes. If a little kid wants to become a professional basketball player, they can't just rely on their visualizations of greatness, watching others, and memorizing plays. If that's all they did, we know what would happen on try-out day. They have to be willing to get out on the court and miss one hundred shots before they can celebrate that first *swish*.

The same goes if you want to be a journalist, a therapist, a meditation teacher, a nurse, or a supportive and loving spouse, parent, or friend. Sure, you can keep pushing away the *doing*, postponing it until you're "ready." But how will you know when you know enough, when you have *enough* information? How will you know when you've planned for *every* contingency? The answer is, you can't. There's always more to learn—and you learn by doing the dang thing.

At various points in my life, I have felt like an imposter cellist, songwriter, spiritual director, Enneagram educator, and activist. Heck, I've even felt like an imposter *adult*. An imposter dog mom. An imposter "healthy person." But the truth is, I'm just a person, experimenting with my life, like everyone else with theirs. I'm not an imposter *anything*. I'm a messy, inconsistent human being who totally knocks it out of the park some days and strikes out on others. And I'm finally okay with that, because at least I'm in the game. But this "okay-ness" with mistakes didn't come easily. I had to work for it. I had to learn what to do when I get pulled over by those pesky Imposter Police who insist on checking my credentials again and again.

The way to get out of an Imposter Police interrogation is to contact your Inner Guidance. This is that still, small voice inside that wants what's *actually* best for you, that wants you to live out your full potential. It can be hard to hear this voice above the racket of the Imposter Police's advice-giving and constant warnings, but it's there. We all have it. Usually, it comes to us not as a voice, but as an inner longing, the restlessness of the soul that feels the call to something more. Our heart's desires are not selfish or unskillful. They are there for a reason: for the evolving of our souls.

Even if your Imposter Police is yakking away full tilt, you can practice listening in for your Inner Guidance. It can also be helpful to think of it as your Inner Loving Parent, Inner Advocate, or Better Angels. Whatever you want to call it, it's there, and it's waiting for you to finally pay some attention to it. When you do this, you are befriending yourself, learning to trust yourself, and wishing yourself the best, most fulfilling life possible.

Part 3 of this book will say more about Inner Advocates and how to contact them. For now, just trust that they are there, and you can listen to them when they are trying to get your attention through inner nudges and longings. Eventually, it is possible to give them more credit and attention than your Inner Critic. Doesn't that sound divine?

YOUR TURN!
Inner Work Exercises

1. Abolish the Imposter Police

Take some time to identify areas of your life where insecurity and self-doubt creep in. Where do the Imposter Police show up to tell you that you don't deserve better, you're not prepared enough, your dreams are too risky, and/or you're sure to fail and make a fool of yourself? Write down all these areas of your life and the messages from the Imposter Police. Then step back and look at them objectively, as if you're witnessing a dear friend say this about themselves. Are these warnings and fears certain to transpire? Sure, they're possible—but are they *likely*? You're a smart cookie, and you probably won't allow the worst of your nightmares to come true. You can practice trusting yourself. There's another crucial step here, and this one's harder—but you can do it! Name these insecurities and doubts *out loud* to a trusted ally, whether that be your best friend, your therapist, a mentor, or a spiritual director. Saying these things out loud helps release them and makes you more aware of them if/when they come back.

2. Listen for Your Heart's Desire

It's there for a reason. Maybe you already know exactly what it is you desire for your lifestyle, career, and relationships. Or maybe you have no clue. That's okay. Right now, you are just *listening inside* for what it is trying to tell you.

Take a moment (at least five minutes) to sit in stillness and silence, and directly ask your heart, "What do you want? What is your deepest desire?" Then wait. Be open and receptive. Don't assume you know the answer. The first things that come to you might be from the ego (e.g., "I wish Billy would hurry up and fall in love with me," "I'd really like to never work another day of my life"). This is wishful, magical thinking, which tends to carry a subtle flavor of tension, resentment, or agitation. When you contact your heart's true desire, there will be a flavor of ease, release, and spaciousness. It will also be of benefit to all those around you.

If all you can contact are the wishes of the ego, then ask yourself, "What is beneath this wish?" For example, if you want to never work another day in your life, perhaps the desire beneath that is actually to quit your job and find more fulfilling work, or to learn how to relax and bring more ease into your life. Don't worry if you feel like you didn't get the "right" answer from your heart immediately. You're just practicing listening to the language of the soul. The answer might not come in words; and it may come days, weeks, or months later. If you keep listening, your heart and soul *will* speak.

And—you guessed it—once your heart does speak to you about its desires, don't keep this to yourself. If it just stays inside your head, it is vulnerable to attacks from the Imposter Police and other Inner Critics. Name it out loud to a trusted ally so that your heart's desire is having a conversation with someone who cares about you and has your best interests in mind. Once your dream is spoken to someone outside of you, it is actually more safe than if you hold it all in. It also gains energy and power when it is spoken aloud, which means it has a fighting chance of becoming reality! Don't hold it in for fear of failure. What is scarier: failing once or twice, or dying after an un-lived life?

3. Search for a Mentor
We're not children anymore, so our parents aren't going to insist we get matched with a mentor from the Boys & Girls Club of America. We've got to take the initiative on our own. It's not as scary as it sounds. Here's all you have to do:

    a. Identify your heart's desire (or one of them).

    b. Look for someone you know who seems to be living your dream (or something like it). You don't have to know them well. If you want to be a beekeeper, who do you know who keeps bees? If you're considering proposing to your partner but are terrified of commitment, who do you know who seems to be in a genuinely happy marriage? If you want to be a professional jazz musician, who is someone you respect and is making their way in the music scene?

c. Invite that person out for coffee or a phone call. Tell them the goals you have and that you really respect the way they navigate themselves in their field. Mention that you'd like to get together with them and ask some questions about how they got started. Chances are they will be extremely flattered and will say yes. You're not being a burden on them. Being asked for advice and guidance is both an ego boost and a joy. (If they say no, don't take it personally. Either they're a jerk, or they just weren't the right fit for you. Contact someone else. Don't be deterred.)

d. Actually *do* the things they suggest as first steps. Then ask them more questions as you go. That's it! Now you have a mentor! Now you're not alone on this journey with only the Imposter Police to give you terrible advice.

CHAPTER 7:
The Locker Room Boys

Doing inner spiritual work alone isn't easy; it's impossible.
—Georges Ivanovitch Gurdjieff

Sitting at the bottom of a long row of concrete steps, I closed my eyes to listen to the shrieks of small children in the wading pool. I couldn't help but smile. We were all finally free from the oppression of winter. The spring air was only fifty-eight degrees, but the sun was unhindered by clouds. That was warm enough for Minnesotan children. They toddled straight into the water without hesitation.

Then, there he was, walking toward me, sunshine bursting from behind him. Evan. I shaded my eyes from the brightness and grinned, trying to play it cool. After all, we had mutual friends, and this wasn't clearly defined as a date.

As we strolled around the lake, it was as if the whole world was born to express this one moment. The energy of the budding trees, the geese's aggressive and silly mating rituals, the mallards laughing simply for the pure joy of arriving back home—even my dog, Chancho, was behaving himself on the leash for once, calmly ambling beside us with his ears laid back in a relaxed posture. Our conversation wove gently in and out between the sacred and the profane. I remember noticing that Evan felt like an old soul trapped inside a young man's body.

Three hours later, the sun was setting with gold and orange hues painting the sky; and the bats had come out of their slumber to feast, giving us a magnificent air show above the water. Evan and I sat and watched. We breathed.

We talked. We sat in silence. We turned every once in a while to smile at each other. I didn't want to leave, and he was making no real moves to get back to the homework from which he was procrastinating. The light sweater I was donning as a backup layer wasn't thick enough against the cool evening air, but it didn't matter. We would draw this first date out as long as possible.

When I arrived home that night, I instantly texted my bestie: "Evan is either going to be my new best friend, or my next lover. He checks all the boxes, I'm attracted to him, AND he's a healthy, balanced person for once! I'm smitten." I had a good feeling about this one. It felt different this time. More grounded.

The next day, I texted Evan, making sure to reiterate that I'd had a good time, I thought he was super cool, and I would love to hang out again soon. I kept it short and sweet. No need to go into full-blown overshare, like I used to when I dated active alcoholics. *Just chill, Chelsea*, I was thinking. *One day at a time. It's only a first date. Turn it over. Godde's got this.*

No response. I waited. Days passed, and fear of my inadequacy grew. I had done something wrong. I fucking blew it—*again*.

Five days later, Evan texted back, "Hey—nice meeting you and Chancho. Thanks for the great conversation. Take care, and I'll see you around."

What. The. Fuck?

How could I have been so far off in my estimation of what that evening meant? My feelings had betrayed me again. Not only did I not accurately read if someone was interested in me, but I also had no idea how to attract a healthy, spiritually and emotionally grounded partner. This confirmed it: I was too broken and codependent to ever be in a healthy relationship.

I kept replaying our goodbye hug. Should I have held on that long? Should I have held on longer? Should I have sounded less enthusiastic to get together again and talk about spirituality? (*Gawd, Chelsea! You are just too intense for men to handle. Back the fuck off. Why do you feel the need to be the aggressor every damn time?*) Did I appear desperate by texting him the following day? Would he have been attracted to me if I had acted more passive? (*You blew it again, dumbass. There will never be another person you're attracted to, and no one is ever going to be into you. You're too much. You're going to die alone and destitute under a bridge.*)

THE LOCKER ROOM BOYS

Somehow, my fears of failed romance always end with me being homeless and chewed on by stray dogs under a bridge. The ridiculousness of that thought usually snaps me back to reality. But the damage has been done. The Locker Room Boys have entered my brain to wreak havoc on my self-esteem. Once their banter starts, it's difficult to turn it off.

I cannot begin to count the many times these douchey assholes have co-opted my self-worth. I am a confident woman, a feminist (meaning that I believe all genders and sexes deserve equal treatment, opportunities, and rights—and yes, it is still necessary to define *feminism* in 2023 *sigh*). I know I am capable, beautiful, and uniquely attractive. But when someone I'm interested in doesn't reciprocate in the way I'd hoped, all of society's sexist and women-blaming messages come flooding in, creating a monster of an Inner Critic that sounds very much like misogynist teenage boys rating girls they've turned down behind the safety of locker room doors. Comparing me to some idealized, photoshopped female body. Dissing my assertive and intelligent nature, my desire for authenticity and transparency, my exuberance for life and sexuality. Everything admirable about my power and presence becomes the perceived reason for rejection.

It didn't help that every time I visited my sweet grandmother, she asked if I had a boyfriend yet. She was clearly distressed each time I showed up single. One time, she even said, "I worry about you. Who is going to take care of you?" When I turned thirty, she stopped asking. She had given up on me. I was now an old maid, destined to be a spinster forever.

My whole life, I've been encouraged by mentors, family, and teachers to be strong, smart, and brave. Then whenever I amazingly arrive at that destination and express my power, it seems I am punished for it. If you are a woman, you already know what I mean. The crushing double standard placed upon us makes it impossible to win. Be sexy, but don't flaunt it. Be intelligent but not a genius, because that will threaten your male colleagues' egos. Be a career woman, but don't advance too far lest you outpace potential mates. Be yourself, but leave your emotions at the door. Be deep and spiritual, but if you get too comfortable with your body and Mother Nature, your witchiness will get you burned at the stake.

True freedom can feel like a pipe dream, yet it calls to us from deep within our bones. The ancient Grandmother Wisdom within desires to shake off the generational layers of patriarchy's wounds, to strip naked under the midday sun and dive headfirst into the ocean of Truth, Presence, and the blessed assurance of unshakable Self-Love.

What would it be like to *truly rest* in the knowing that there is an infinite source that is the Source of all contentedness, all causeless joy, all ease, all acceptance? To accept reality as it shows up in each moment? To accept *myself*, even when I feel like damaged goods or like I've blown my chances again? I catch fleeting glimpses of this state of being, and that has been enough for me to fall in love with its pursuit. Of course, chasing and striving are not the path. However, wanting to experience the loving quality of equanimity no matter the circumstances is a wholesome desire—and a good place to start. With that desire, extensive progress can be made. I am living proof.

My dating history is a great place to measure the progression of my self-worth. Without boring you with detailed accounts of my calloused thought streams of self-hatred, I'll attempt to list all the reasons I've deemed myself unworthy of love, intimacy, and committed partnership. (I'll skip high school, because, duh, we were all insecure in our teenage dating escapades.)

During my first year in college, I dumped my wonderful boyfriend to keep chasing my high school crush, even though I knew that he was mentally unstable and an addict and that it wouldn't work out. (*You're not capable of settling down. You're too in love with the chase. You don't even have the sense to stick with a good thing when it's in the palm of your hand.*)

A month later, I found my "soulmate." Someone totally new. There he was, in the middle of the campus quad, teaching a graffiti workshop, with sagging pants and his shiny black hair sparkling in the sun. He was visiting for a few days from California, quietly indoctrinating nineteen-year-old Iowans in the creative art of street prophecy and rebellion. He was a genius. The spray can in his hand created colorful worlds that seemed to pop right off the wall. I'm sure his younger, more handsome brother stole the show for most of the onlookers, with his interpersonal banter and constant jokes. But I only had eyes for Jax.

His quietness drew me in, and I wanted to understand the depth behind his dark eyes and dopey grin.

Jax became my everything over the next four years. At the end of my first year in college, I spent a month with him in the inner city of San Bernardino, and it changed the course of my life. I was suddenly exposed to a new side of America, one filled with unequal opportunities for Black and brown folks. Addiction, incarceration, teenage pregnancies, gang activity, police brutality, disease, and poverty were on every block, oppressing every family. I was suddenly a foreigner in my own country, but Jax showed me the ropes. He helped me understand, helped me fit in. We stayed up late every night in his room, sharing our stories, laughing, crying, making art, and listening to music. He was the first man to kiss me on my neck, and it awakened something in me I didn't know was there: repressed desires that longed to be expressed. And yet I resisted. I told him I was waiting until marriage, to which he smiled and replied, "Well then, I guess I am too."

The plane ride back to Minnesota at the end of that month felt like a death. I cried through the whole flight. Our long-distance relationship of late-night ramblings on the phone devolved into me trying to counsel him out of his drug addictions. The stress built as I forgave his infidelity in my dramatic gestures of martyrdom. I just couldn't let go. He was my *soulmate*, after all. How could I abandon him to his cycles of depression, existential angst, and the oppressions of addiction? When he began smoking crack, I finally raised the white flag, hating myself for my selfishness. (*You were just too weak to help him. Maybe if you would have offered yourself sexually instead of being such a prude, things would have worked out. Now you'll never find another love that is that magical.*)

Magical? Looking back, it was 20 percent fun and 80 percent torture!

Then there was Gregg, who convinced me I was too old to be a virgin at age twenty-three—and, thus, undatable. (*How could you have been so stupid as to listen to those abstinence-only thumpers? Now you've missed your window of deflowering opportunity!*)

(Actually, Gregg was just a coward and had his own twisted view on sexuality. And I'd had no alternative views on sexuality presented to me up until that point. So how could I have chosen differently?)

A series of alcoholics followed—all of them truly wonderful people at heart, underneath their addictive behaviors. Each time I discovered their addiction, I berated myself. (*What the heck is wrong with you? Why didn't you see this coming? You're doomed to date alcoholics for the rest of your life, so you might as well give up now.*)

I had a good thing with party boy David, until he told me I wasn't attractive enough to him because I wore baggy pants. Vance cut me out because I made him uncomfortable about being poor by taking him out to a fancy restaurant. I lost the glorious heart connection with dear Ezra when I refused to convert to Judaism for his mother. I pushed anxious Stephen into intimacy too fast by offering to help him figure out his Enneagram type. I could have had a chance with that hot barista James or that sexy librarian Kai—if I had been willing to try out polyamory. And I freaked out Josiah by sharing that I have a deep love for Jesus. Each time a relationship or a developing crush petered out, I assumed it didn't work out because of me. (*I'm too old/scrawny/spiritual/smart/aggressive/prudish/demanding/broken to have a partner. I'm unattractive! Doomed! A flawed excuse for a female! I'd internally bang my head against the metaphorical wall of sexual and domestic failure.*)

Looking back at all these scenarios, it's clear that I was not at fault for these breakups. Of course, I was a participant, and I played a role. But strikingly, my role was more about believing the lie of my unworthiness than actually making mistakes that caused people to leave me.

It seems the Universe knew I needed one more horrendously painful relationship to finally wake me up from my sense of unworthiness, martyrdom, codependency, and self-defeating patterns. This lesson came in the form of Timothy Anderson, another "soulmate" who I held on to for way too long. (I'll call him T, my real nickname for him, from this point forward.)

Listening to T talk about furry animals was my favorite pastime. Or he could be talking about the emerging science of neuroplasticity. Or how plain ol' black pepper is the best spice, despite T's ingenuity and prodigy in the kitchen. Any of these topics would start his big hands flapping, lightly fluttering back and forth as the pace of his speech quickened to a manic tilt. Grinning from ear to ear, his green eyes alive with excitement, he would now be on a roll, unable to stop: "And then the little Frenchie started sneezing repeatedly, and when he finally stopped, he looked around in a brief daze, and then shyly wagged his tail because that little pupper enjoys the satisfaction of a good sneeze just like any of us, and my heart exploded and I just needed to squish him with all of my love!"

Eventually, T would run out of breath and gasp for air, clutching at his chest in a fit of giggles. It was the giggles that I was truly waiting for. The content of the story made no nevermind. The schoolboy giggles emanating from this gorgeous human's huge emotions were always worth the wait—and I would wait forever to witness those moments.

Whenever I got angry, I'd cuss a blue streak, either in my head or out through my mouth. T had the most creative way of gently knocking me off my high horse in a way no one else could. He wasn't afraid of my anger.

"Can you believe this *stupid-ass* telephone?" I'd say, slamming the malfunctioning piece of shit onto the table.

"No, I can't," T would calmly respond. "I didn't know they made stupid *ass telephones*." His slight change of inflection on my original phrase would always throw my rant off its tracks; and we'd fly into a fit of guffaws, imagining someone's ass talking into a telephone.

Those joy-filled moments were abundant, which was why we eventually talked of marriage on our road trip out west. I had never known a love like this. But even more copious were the moments filled with dread, confusion, irritation, self-doubt, and paranoia. These are the emotions that inevitably accompany a relationship with an actively drinking alcoholic.

T couldn't help his backslide into relapse time and again. That's what addiction is, after all: an uncontrollable dependence upon a substance, accompanied by denial, obsession, and psychological and physical cravings. In the two years we were together, he couldn't go more than two months without binge-drinking. I didn't understand. I thought there was someone at fault. I would either blame and shame T for falling off the wagon, or blame myself for not keeping him from relapsing. We went round and round, spinning into darkness, isolation, and fear. I spent all my time with him, hovering and mothering, trying to protect him from his poor choices. I left behind all my hobbies, interests, and joys. In my mind, there was only T and the fear of relapse, a black storm cloud that blotted out the sun that was our love.

When I finally jumped off the hellish carousel, empowered by the grace of Godde and the proddings of a dear friend, I landed my ass in a Twelve Step community that intimately understood my dysfunction. Being ever the good student, I found myself a sponsor within the first three months, because I read and was told that was the best way to "work the program." I chose Greta because she was brutally honest in her sharing and could laugh at herself. I needed to learn those skills. I also chose her because she had amazing dreadlocks.

We met together at Dunn Brothers Coffee week after week, with me sharing my story, feelings, and anxieties. She would listen carefully, take a moment of silence, and then share her relevant experience on what she had learned on the matter, offering me tools from the program to practice that week. She didn't judge me. Eventually, I shared my doubts about leaving T. Was it the right choice? Was it selfish of me? Should I have waited it out? Stayed true to our commitment? Would I ever find another love that felt so deep and authentic? What if I screwed up Godde's plan for my life by leaving him? I had stopped believing in soulmates after parting ways with Jax, but my karma felt so intertwined with T's that I couldn't fully justify leaving him, even though being with him made me feel like I was losing my mind. (*But you promised you'd love him forever. You're a flake. A floozy. Always on to the next thing. Selfish bitch.*)

Then Greta said something to me that cracked a hole in the Locker Room Boys' arguments and changed my life: "You can't screw it up. If you're meant to be together, you will be. And if you're *not* meant to be together, you can't mess that up either. There are larger forces at play here than just your individual will, Chelsea."

Such a simple concept. It has shifted my outlook on everything, like whether to accept a job offer, get a dog, or move across the country. I can never have all the information about something, but I can always change course if my intuition is telling me to. Future doors will open. Future doors will close. All have a way of dancing with the "meant to be." Claiming I'm trusting the flow of life and actually surrendering to it are two separate things. While my self-blame around T had lessened, it still crept in on me almost daily.

A few months after this talk with Greta, I was doing some gentle yoga in my living room, trying to ease my stress levels and my monkey mind, when a muscle in my mid-back suddenly clenched up with a painful twist. Being taught by my spiritual director to consult Louise Hay's list of physical symptoms and their corresponding mental and emotional catalyzers each time a new pain or sickness appeared, I pulled out the list in the book *You Can Heal Your Life*. I doubt that this method is 100 percent accurate all the time—and yet I was astounded by what I found. It was spot-on.

"Middle-back issues . . . The probable cause: 'Guilt. Stuck in all that *stuff* back there. Get off my back!'[7]" Yep. I wanted to be free of that baggage. Next to this was a new thought pattern that heals this pattern: "I release the past. I am free to move forward with love in my heart."[8] My shame was manifesting physically. If I couldn't forgive myself or T, I knew the pain would only get worse.

I gathered up everything in my house that was connected to T with the intent to get rid of it all. I needed a physical ritual of release and energetic cleansing. So I burned all of our letters, pictures, and paintings. I also deleted our emails, blocked him on Facebook, and deleted his number from my phone. I was doing this not out of spite, but for my own highest good. Then I wrote him a letter of amends, listing all the things I had learned from him and all I was grateful for from our time together. I also cut up a shirt his mom had given me for Christmas and sewed it into a string of prayer flags, writing the name of each person in T's family on each cloth square.

Next, I grabbed the letter, the prayer flags, and several pairs of earrings T had given me and biked down to the Mississippi River. Finding a secluded spot among the oaks and maples, I strung the flags through their branches. These trees would hold my prayers and ensure they continued. With tears streaming down my face, I chucked the earrings as far out into the water as I could. I listened for a splash but heard none. They just slipped out of sight. Collapsing onto a downed tree, I sat and read aloud my letter of amends. Taking a deep breath and saying a quick prayer of forgiveness, I burned it. Mixed its ashes in with the sandy riverbank. (Due to the unstable nature of T's addiction and behaviors at that point, my sponsor had advised that I not send the letter or contact him in person, as a way to ensure my safety and his.)

From that day forward, whenever the Locker Room banter entered my head with thoughts like *You screwed it up*, I easily noticed it and sent myself some love. *It's not your fault, Chelsea*, I'd think. *You didn't know any better at that time. And neither did T. You can't control him or cure him, and you certainly didn't cause his condition. You are good. You are beautiful. You are healing.*

Years later, my new sponsor, Sharon, taught me something else when Evan rejected me. When I told her I was really confused and sad about his response, she said, "Of course you are! That's a really confusing situation! And you have every right to feel that way. The secret is to *allow* yourself to feel this. Just sit with it and nurture it for a while instead of beating yourself up. Feel the grief and confusion, both from the situation itself *and* from the time lost to listening to that nasty Inner Voice."

This was the missing ingredient. Having rejected the inner Locker Room talk, I needed something with which to replace it. Surprise, surprise—that replacement is always compassion. You just cannot go wrong with kindness. Can you imagine a single situation where it is not possible or appropriate to respond with kindness? Sure, it's easy to imagine situations where it is difficult to respond in this way. But *impossible*? Some scenarios might require fierceness and firmness (e.g., in responding to bullying or systemic oppression), but that doesn't mean compassion cannot also be present. They do not cancel each other out.

So often, our Inner Critic attacks us when we're already in a difficult moment. As if the situation were not hard enough, the Inner Critic feels it is somehow helpful to hurl layers of doubt, insults, and cruel stories into the mix. This is the "second dart" of self-criticism and blame that is referenced in Buddhist teachings. The metaphor is this: Life has already shot an arrow of suffering at us, and then we shoot *ourselves* in the foot by making it personal, thinking things like, *See, you had this coming*, *You deserve this*, or *You weren't smart enough to avoid this*. Oftentimes, a third dart will impale us when we then judge ourselves for judging ourselves. And then around and around we go.

Whether married, partnered, divorced, or single, humans find ways to suffer in relationships. Perhaps because human beings are complicated, relationships will always be messy. But that doesn't mean we have to add further layers of suffering by creating stories about our inadequacy, replaying our screwups, or feeding moods that keep us down in the dumps. No reason to shoot yourself with that proverbial "second dart" when you're already experiencing the pain of grief, confusion, or anger. When in those unavoidable moments, may we all employ our inner angels, breathe deeply, and call upon Kindness to lead the way home.

Sometimes Kindness is best served with a healthy dose of assertive boundaries. It was time for me to stand up for myself against these bullying boys, so I wrote them this letter:

Dear Locker Room Bros,

Dudes, it's hard being a teenage boy. There is so much pressure to conform, to be masculine and tough—which usually means acting like a jerk. You've said a lot of things you didn't mean and regretted it. Especially what you've said about women—about their bodies, their intelligence, their emotions. You rate them on a scale of 1 to 10. You laugh behind girls' backs to impress your friends.

But I know you. You're not a misogynist, not an asshole. What you are is scared and insecure, and that's a hard place to be. Under it all is a fear that you'll never find the love you dream of in secret, and a fear that you will find that love and you won't be worthy of it.

There's only one way to become worthy of it, one way to start living without regrets for your internalized chauvinism, one way to open yourself up to real love: Stop degrading, devaluing, rating, and harassing women. I don't like it. Nobody likes it. Show some respect. I will not tolerate your abuse any longer.

In addition, show some respect to yourself. You are a good person. So act like it. You will need to stop giving authority to your friends, your sexist grandpa, and the surgically altered and airbrushed superstars in Hollywood. You must become your own authority. You. You have a right to feel and express your emotions and to have them be received with love—your fear, your insecurities, your confusion, your frustration. They don't make you any less manly. They make you more human.

It is safe to express your feelings, bro. Let's talk. But only if you are respectful. If not, you leave.

Your friend, with firm boundaries,
Chelsea

YOUR TURN!
Inner Work Exercises

1. Verbalize Your Inner Critic of Self-Blame and Insecurity to a Trusted Ally
I've said this before, and I'll say it again, since this cannot be overstated: Your trusted ally can be a therapist, a mentor, a sponsor, a spiritual director, or a friend. I know how scary it can be to work up the courage to do so, but it will have great payoffs when done in a safe space with someone you know will not judge you or try to immediately fix you. In Twelve Step programs, they say, "We're only as sick as our secrets," and it's true. When they are held inside, they fester and grow (often subconsciously) into a demon that can block our healing. Speaking our silly fears, twisted views of self, and crippling shame out loud takes away the power of the secret. Once we hear it and someone else witnesses it, it no longer feels like such a big deal. It can even sound humorous. The other person can mirror back the ridiculousness of your beliefs and give you an alternative voice and message to practice.

I wish I could say that just verbalizing your Inner Demons to yourself in the mirror had the same medicinal effect. It does not. Mysteriously, humans were made to heal through relationships. We are social animals. As Georges Gurdjieff so precisely stated, "Doing inner spiritual work alone isn't easy; it's impossible!" The sooner we can embrace this, the sooner we are on the path toward wholeness.

2. Create a Ritual of Release Around "Stuck Areas" in Your Life
What does your mind return to again and again with blame, shame, regret, or confusion? Is there some puzzle you are trying to piece back together to make

sense of it all? Have you been around this particular hamster wheel for the thousandth time? Perhaps it's time to let go.

Just saying "let go" usually isn't enough. Put some time and intention into creating a ritual of release. Are there any objects that represent this situation for you? Gather them up and decide how to release them through regifting, burning, burying, shredding, or smashing. Call on something greater than yourself to help you release this pain. Then smash it. Burn it. Chuck it in the river (if it won't affect the water quality!). Write out all your feelings without censorship and make sure to include what you have learned from the situation. Gratitude is key. It releases resentment to notice how this situation has actually helped you grow. Burn some incense. Sing a song. Do it alone, with a single witness, or with a circle of friends who are also releasing their pain. As long as you commit to being kind to yourself through the whole process, you can't do it wrong.

Get as weird as you'd like. Ask for guidance in knowing what to include in the ritual. Brainstorm ideas with a friend. If no clear inspiration comes, just do something anyway. Get the stuck energy moving, and more required actions may be revealed in the future. When your mind tries to jump back on its familiar hamster wheel, the memory of your ritual will help you notice this thought with love and help you hop off the wheel.

CHAPTER 8:
Satan and the Street Preacher

Anger is murderously sweet.
—The Buddha

Fifteen minutes into the movie I was watching, I could feel my jaw clenching, the irritation in my body expanding beyond the physical limits of my skin. Perhaps this ode to chauvinism would somehow manage to redeem itself. Jonathan sat beside me, happily munching away on his jumbo popcorn. He offered me some; I shook my head. My stomach had no room for food. There was a monster down there, ripping apart my insides.

As the plot began to wrap up, I was berating myself for sitting through this shit. Physically trembling, I had to concentrate just to get myself to walk from the theater to the car, my breathing quick and shallow. Having watched the whole thing through to the end, I could construct a legitimate argument about how this common narrative perpetuates violence toward women. Just one more chick flick where the strong, independent woman falls for the very man she hates at the beginning of the film: the misogynist player who sleeps around, talks about her cup size to his buddies, and has a habit of telling her, "Relax. You should smile more. Your angry face is really a boner-killer." And then she falls for him because he buys her a dozen roses. Fuck that.

"Did you like it?" Jonathan asked, unlocking the car doors.

"Are you fucking kidding me? Did *you*?"

"I thought it was cute."

The creature in my belly began clawing its way up my esophagus, pressing against my windpipe. I tried to take a deep breath before laying out my rational explanation of why this trash heap of a story was brainwashing men into thinking sexism is sexy, perpetuating the endless cycles of oppression against me and my sisters.

"It's just a story," Jonathan said, merging the car onto the freeway. "You're overreacting."

The demon in me finally wrenched its way from my esophagus and out of my mouth, the flavor of bile spewing into my words. The more I lectured, the more defiant Jonathan became. I couldn't stop it. My vision was blurred by the white-hot flashes exploding before my eyes. I blacked out, unable to remember any specifics about the vitriol spewing from within me. When I came to, I found myself pounding my fist against Jonathan's head. "You! Are! The reason! Women! Are! Being! Murdered!"

The words flew out in an abrupt staccato with each bang of my fist. Jonathan was trying to deflect me while keeping one hand on the wheel as we careened down the highway at seventy miles per hour. By some miracle, he managed to not swerve off the road and plow us headlong into a tree. We both survived my demonic possession. At some point during my assault, I miraculously had an out-of-body experience and saw myself punching my friend. It scared me enough to quickly pull out of the argument.

"You're hopeless," I said eventually. "You'll never understand anyway."

Jonathan was happy to let it lie at that. Needless to say, we never hung out again. Just one more friendship killed by my need to be right, to win. By my incapability of listening to any view or life experience different from my own. By my tirades, lectures, and insistence that people educate themselves (with my approved sources of information). Surprisingly, Jonathan refriended me on Facebook after eight years of radio silence. He probably wanted to check if I was in prison for murder yet.

One night, at 12:13 a.m., my eyes snapped open. My heart was pounding in my chest. I recognized why instantly. It wasn't a bad dream that had woken me. It was my hyperactive mind, grinding out arguments on an issue to prove to myself that I am right: *Think about it from every angle. They're going to come at you with this argument, and you need to be ready to respond. Always be one step ahead!*

Feeling my body sinking into the comfy hotel mattress and down pillows, I desperately wanted to go back to sleep. But I was sweating, my breathing elevated. I was at a four-day spiritual direction conference, and I needed to conserve my energy for the full day ahead. *Please, God, not this shit again,* I begged. It had been twelve years since I'd almost forced Jonathan off the road while seeing red, but the same voice was back. While I had managed not to hit anyone since then, this demon still visited me about once every year.

Oh yeah, baby! the Inner Voice said. *Here we go! I'm right! You're right, and we have to prove it to these morally bankrupt imbeciles masquerading as spiritual directors! How could they possibly be advocating for polyamory? These people are supposed to be the enlightened ones! Bunch of new age posers!*

I tried to bring some calm into my body and some space into my mind by bringing my attention to my breath. I was familiar enough with this voice to know better than to argue with it. That only made it stronger. But the voice in my head was too loud to keep my attention on my breath for more than one inhale. It continued to pontificate, slinging arguments, research, examples, and references about how these people were choosing the dishonest and dangerous path in life.

I flipped over onto my other side. Maybe I'd be more comfortable in this position.

You can't let them get away with this! the Inner Voice continued. *It's either hell in a hand basket for our society, or a really fun ride that you're going to be left out of. So we've gotta rein in these floozies!*

The day before, I had led a workshop on spirituality, gender, and sexuality; and someone had asked for clarification and thoughts around polyamory and open relationships. I remained calm on the surface. But internally, I panicked. A few participants stepped in to answer—one a pastor, the other a Zen priestess—to share their positive personal experiences with polyamory.

Now, lying in bed, the clock reading 1:15 a.m., I kept reliving this scene and creating new conversations in my head, situations where I would come out on top, arguments I would win about how open relationships are disastrous and monogamy is the only way to be in a healthy relationship with the self and with others. I was stuck. Intellectually, I was ready to let go of "my way or the highway" on this issue. Honestly, I could imagine that some people found polyamory to be fulfilling and navigated it in a respectful, healthy way. But emotionally, I was still being triggered by the handful of people in open relationships who had personally hurt me with their lies—people who had chosen not to tell me I wasn't the only one they were dating.

Nothing was working: not prayer, not any of my meditation tricks, none of my "Dharma moves." I just wanted the voice to shut up and leave me alone. I was so sick of this knot of righteousness within me. I couldn't care less how that pastor or that priestess had chosen to conduct their dating life. Their choices had nothing to do with me. And yet something within me was feeling threatened and vulnerable.

I realized I couldn't win against the Inner Voice. He was on his soapbox, and there was only one thing that was going to get him to stop ranting. So I grabbed my journal and a pen, then crept out into the hallway, careful not to wake my roommate. I needed to get to the bottom of my Rage Demon once and for all. It was time to get to know this character instead of trying in vain to push him away.

It was already a given that this Inner Voice was a man. The energy behind his hatred could never be labeled as feminine. Setting an intention to remain open and curious, I put my pen to paper, asking the Inner Voice who he was and what he was trying to accomplish. As I wrote down his common phrases and arguments, it became clear that he was always shouting through a megaphone, even to the point that he was so loud there was no room for any calm, dispassionate thought to enter my mind. As I looked back at all the times I had flown into a rage trying to prove myself right, I noticed his talking style was one-sided preaching.

That's it! I thought. It all came crashing together in an instant, all my horrible memories of pushing away people I loved through my lecturing and pontificating. I was like the person you avoid on the downtown street corner. *My God. I have an inner Street Preacher!* A wave of relief crashed over me. Just naming him instantly released his grip on my intestines. The tight clench around my heart loosened, and I began to weep. Compassion for my years of entrenched self-righteousness seeped through my bones like grateful crops receiving rain after a drought.

I knew the path to freedom had finally opened. I was free to detach from this demon, to just walk right past him on the street without paying him any mind—or tell him, "Jesus already loves you. You don't have to do this," and *then* keep on walking. This was the Demon that had caused me the most pain and separation in my life, my most deep-seated Inner Critic. I pictured him instantly as an unassuming, clean-cut, white evangelical preacher: my childhood authority, the thing I loved and feared most.

I asked him what his motivation was and how he was trying to help me. *I'm protecting you from falling astray!* the Street Preacher said. *Keeping you on the straight and narrow, the moral high ground. Out of trouble, safe from sin!* With some more probing, it became clear that he was protecting me from the sting of being *wrong,* because I had come to equate wrong with *bad.* As long as I could have a solid argument and come out on top, I was right and, therefore, good. Above reproach. No black marks on *this* soul, thank you very much!

Ironically, most of the darkest blots on my conscience have been caused by the Street Preacher. He ended up marring me with the very thing he was trying to protect me against. Every time his anger flared up and I attempted to maintain my integrity to my values by educating someone who was lost in their ignorance, I ended up falling out of my integrity. I would be cruel, harsh, and dismissive of others' experiences. I ended up acting like the *bad* person I was lecturing others against.

That night, after I came to this realization, a deep sadness set in. It was a grief I had never known. I had wasted so much time letting my irritation with the world eat away at my body, clenching the muscles of my back, jaw, and pelvic floor into a therapeutic mess. I had let this Inner Voice put distance between me and my loved ones, making me into a dangerous person who was not to be trusted when all I wanted was to help them see the light.

SATAN AND THE STREET PREACHER

The Street Preacher had been there during my junior year of high school, when I found myself ripping my friend Dave's character to shreds after I found out he was an atheist. At some point, I sat down and realized the whole cafeteria had been staring at me. The Preacher had also been there in all of my well-structured lectures against US militarism that were aimed at Cory, who had spent his career in various forms of criminal justice and law enforcement. It had never occurred to me that if these jobs needed to exist, it was best that they were filled by calm, gentle, loving people like Cory. Instead, I had lumped him in with the enemy, even though he had been part of the solution. When I finally asked Cory how my years of preaching had affected him, he shared that he had mostly learned to nod his head and keep his opinions and experiences to himself. He said he had felt shut down and unheard. My brother is the person I love most in this world, and my insistence on speaking to him from a soapbox had removed any chance at true intimacy we could have had throughout my twenties.

In addition, the Street Preacher had been there when I had written a letter outlining all the counterarguments against the Bush-era absurdity, as I slipped it into my dad's Bill O'Reilly book before heading back to college after winter break. And he had been there when I'd dropped my first *f*-bomb in front of my parents. ("I don't want to follow any God who tortures his children for eternity! That's some fucking sadistic, abusive shit!") Mom had brought her "How to Convert Muslims" pamphlets into my house so she could study its tactics. Poor Dad had kept trying to divert my attention back to our wood project out in the garage, but I hadn't been smart enough to take the bait. Instead, I had stood my ground until I'd crushed Mom's spirit and all she had held dear. (Sure, I still heartily disagree with her. But did I have to shout, swear, and berate her? It didn't help the situation or change her mind.) I had probably done it to atone for my teenage sin of demolishing Dave for being an atheist. Round and round, I hadn't known how to step off this hellish merry-go-round.

The Street Preacher is best buddies with another Inner Voice, one without whom he could not do his work: Satan the Accuser. Let me be clear: I don't believe in any literal incarnation of evil, no Devil with horns and a pitchfork who rules the realm of Hell and strategically tempts good people into straying from the path. Naw. But he is a helpful metaphor for our ego, our bad habits, and the human propensity to cause harm over and over again.

One of the most common nicknames for Satan is the Accuser. He's always running around, pointing fingers at someone else, never taking responsibility for his part in the matter. Some people interpret the snake in the Garden of Eden to be Satan. The snake certainly taught the original humans a new behavior: blaming and shaming. Adam blamed Eve, Eve blamed the serpent, and the serpent originally blamed God but is nowhere to be found at the end of the story. He slithered away while man and woman stood bickering.

I've done that too—many times. I slithered away from blame. It's so easy to see how deluded and irrational other people are acting. It's so easy to see how they are hurting themselves with their ignorance or their refusal to look at their patterns, motivations, and fantasies. It's so easy for me to want to get right in there and fix them, teach them, give them the right tools, and prove that I'm right and helpful and good. For most of my life, that was exactly what I did. I had an ongoing savior complex, thinking I had the solution to all the world's problems. This explains why I had such a long-standing record of dating alcoholics and addicts. *They* needed help, not me; and something in me was compelled to fix them. We fit together hand in glove.

The addict's girlfriend was a convenient position to be in, because changing others and turning them into my pet project was a sure way to get the focus off my defects of character, off my pain. Thinking of new strategies to get my partner sober was, while stressful, easier than looking in the mirror and doing my own inner work. It took a whole parade of alcoholic partners before it dawned on me: *I'm the problem here! Me!* I was the only constant in every relationship equation, and they all played out similarly. My partner and I would end up resenting each other. I resented them for not conforming to my grand plan for their life, a plan that involved healthy choices and sobriety. They resented me for imposing a grand plan on to their life—and for being a controlling know-it-all, manipulating them with my emotional displays. I got to play the role of "caring, stable girlfriend," and I rubbed their noses in the fact that they were playing the role of "stupid, immature, pain-in-the-ass

SATAN AND THE STREET PREACHER

partner." Some of them internalized this shame and stuck around for a while. The smarter ones got really pissed at me, then broke up with me by dating someone else.

Satan the Accuser has gotten me into so many painful scenarios, blocking my capability to see my patterns. It was always someone else's fault. Someone else was always the sick one, not me. Not goody-two-shoes, straight-and-narrow little ol' me!

Jesus directly addressed this deluded way of thinking and acting in his famous Sermon on the Mount. In Matthew 7:3–5, he says this:

> Why do you look at the speck of sawdust in your brother's eye and pay no attention to the plank in your own eye? How can you say to your brother, 'Let me take the speck out of your eye,' when all the time there is a plank in your own eye? You hypocrite, first take the plank out of your own eye, and then you will see clearly to remove the speck from your brother's eye!

Similarly, the Twelve Step community has a saying: "Let it begin with me." When we put this slogan into practice, miracles happen. My whole life, I had been resentful and saddened that my parents never said "I love you." They were the grown-ups! Why couldn't they model vulnerable behavior? I was certain they loved me, that they were good parents. But sharing mushy things like feelings was not a part of our family culture. I kept waiting for them to say it, then complained when they didn't.

Then, one day, my Twelve Step sponsor Greta asked me, "Why don't *you* just say it? You're a part of the family. So if you start saying it, the family culture has changed."

But expecting the child to lead the way is totally unfair! "What if they don't say it back?" I asked.

"So what? At least you won't regret not saying it. Who knows? Maybe they're waiting for you to say it first!"

Fine. I would give it a try. I decided I would say "I love you" after every phone call and visit, no matter how my parents responded. By the third phone call, my dad was cheerfully saying it before I would! He even said it in person when we next saw each other. I was floored. This was the same father who had told me with exasperation ten years earlier, "I just can't change. I wasn't raised to share personal things or feelings, and I'm not going to start now!"

Now, I can see clearly that his changed response was in correlation to my approach. My younger self blamed our distant relationship on him. *He* was the one who had been emotionally repressed and guarded. *He* was the one who had refused to share anything real or meaningful, keeping things on the surface. So I decided to do the same. Why should I put myself out there if he wasn't going to? Once he demonstrated an interest in getting to know me, then I would reciprocate. So we had been at a standoff, too set in our ways to break out of our father-daughter dance.

My Twelve Step friends taught me, though, that I am the one responsible for my actions and that other people are responsible for theirs. Just because someone else is acting poorly doesn't give me a free pass to stoop to their level. No one else's choices reflect poorly on me, even if those people are my parents or my romantic partners. Their choices reflect on *them*. But I hadn't known that. So I had set about my task of trying to fix them, with Satan the Accuser whispering into my ear, instead of changing myself. I hadn't known any better. I had been doing the best I could with what I had been given. And so had they. We all are. At all times.

When I first realized the magnitude of time and energy I had lost trying to "help" other people (aka pointing out their errors and trying to change them), a wave of grief washed over me. There was so much of my life I couldn't get back now. All my years of denial about what I could and could not change had robbed me of the possibility of contentment and happiness. I had been fighting an impossible battle. I hadn't understood that the only person I could change was myself.

I needed to forgive all the people I had tried to help for not changing their ways. They weren't ready. Forgiveness takes time. So I was really angry at myself for doing the same delusional things over and over. But what I needed was to forgive myself.

When I was getting ready to be confirmed in my Lutheran church at age fifteen, we were all told to choose a mentor, someone to talk to about our spiritual and theological questions. I chose my choir teacher, Jane, who had been an example of patience and love for much of my childhood.

At one point, Jane asked me, "Why do you suppose we are told to forgive those who have hurt us?"

Without thought or hesitation, I answered, "Forgiveness isn't for the other person. It's for ourselves. If we hold on to grudges, we get bitter and unhappy."

To this day, I don't know where I got that answer. No one had taught me that. By the surprised look on Jane's face, it certainly wasn't the answer she was expecting either. She told me that she had never thought of this . . . and that she supposed I was right. It's a bummer that I didn't know how to take my own teenage advice for the next twenty years. Forgiveness is hard for anyone, especially for a person who is a master grudge holder. Little by little, I began seeing the truth of the weight of resentment. Holding on to painful memories and replaying them only hurts me, not the other person. As the Buddha once said, "You will not be punished for your anger; you will be punished *by* your anger."

In all of the finger-pointing, grudge-holding, and refusing to change until others changed first, the person who hurt me the most was *me*. I had been fumbling around for years with a plank in my eye, bumping into my addiction to fixing others, only to turn around and bump into it again.

To forgive myself, I had to see clearly what I had been doing wrong—and that was painful to look at. To take personal responsibility, I needed to build up a more loving relationship with myself so that I wouldn't revert to my old patterns of shaming and hating myself after seeing my habits clearly. I also needed to build up a more trusting relationship with something greater than myself, with a Higher Power. If I could have changed of my own volition, I would have done so long ago. I needed help.

Forgiving myself also opens up the possibility for change. Am I ready for that? Sometimes it's easier to hold on to my old ways of thinking, to let the committee of Inner Critics run the show. Forgiveness means trying on new

SATAN AND THE STREET PREACHER

ways of being and changing one's behavior. Saying "I love you" first. Acting in a way that results in self-respect.

It was time for me to speak kindly to all parts of myself, even those personified by Satan:

What up, Satan? I see you.

You've been busy. This world is a big ol' fat mess because no one seems to know how to take responsibility for their thoughts, words, and deeds. They blame the Republicans, the Democrats, the immigrants. Or their spouse, their kids, or their parents. They blame the ignorant masses or the educated elites.

There I go, using they instead of I. You tricked me again, you sneaky Devil!

I used to work at a Bible camp where we would sing a song about stomping on Satan. I couldn't remember the song, so I tried to look it up on YouTube. I was shocked to find at least a dozen different songs about stomping on your head, most of them sung by children. "Put him under your feet!" they joyfully exclaim.

No wonder you're such a meanie. I would be too, if people were kicking me in the head all the time. It must be hard not to blame everyone else for your pain when mobs of children are chasing you and thrashing you on every street corner. As they say, "Hurt people hurt people," and I suppose you're no exception.

From here on out, no more stomping. When you show up wagging your finger all over the place, I will reach out and hold your hand, because I know you're scared. I wish you healing and a clear vision of your faults so that you can forgive yourself. Maybe someday you'll even remember that you are a fallen angel. That's your True Self, and it's how I see you: a lost angel, trying to find his way Home. Your path home is an Inner Journey into the depths of your Shadow, those places within you where you are too afraid to look. Bringing the focus off others and back onto yourself is the Way.

I will not hate you. I will love you into healing.

May you be happy, courageous in the Truth, and free from children's cruel feet.

Your accomplice no more, but your friend forever,
Chelsea

PS: I forgive you.

YOUR TURN!
Inner Work Exercises

1. Forgiveness Practice: "Who Is This Resentment Hurting Right Now?"
Forgiveness is about clearing out the inner clutter so that there is room for acceptance, understanding, and (eventually) love. It doesn't even need to be motivated by *trying* to love the other person. That doesn't work. This is about loving *ourselves* enough to let that shit go. We needn't condone mistreatment or abuse to do this. No need to be a doormat. We can maintain or establish strong protective boundaries as part of the process. This is about not giving away our power and happiness to others. And yes, sometimes it is about remembering that the other person is human and has the right to make mistakes, just like we do. Follow these steps to get started in your forgiveness process, remembering that it is a *process,* and not a magical, instant cure:

   a. Make a list of who you feel resentment toward and why.

   b. Order the list from "Easiest to forgive" to "No way in hell am I forgiving them!"

   c. Start your forgiveness practice with the *easiest* person on your list. Once you feel that energy clear out, then move on to the next person.

   d. Allow yourself to actually *feel* the hurt, anger, fear, or resentment (and even the hatred!) toward each person. Notice its impact on your body, heart, and mind. What type of person do you become when you hold on to this story? Jot down what you notice, and take a moment to send yourself some compassion for this suffering.

e. Present your intention to Godde, the Universe, or your Higher Self, calling in assistance from something greater than your ego. (The ego *loves* holding on to these stories, which keep it alive.) Remember, if we could have forgiven each person already on our own, we would have. It's time to ask for help from something greater than ourselves. Say your intention out loud: "I am willing to forgive _____ and relieve myself from this suffering." If that doesn't feel genuine, amend it to something like this: "I am *willing to become willing* to forgive _____."

f. Breathing in and out, repeat some phrases of forgiveness in your mind or out loud to each person: "To the best of my capability, I forgive you. My heart is willing to release this hurt, for my own highest good. I forgive you, knowing that you are also a wounded person in need of release." (You can make up other phrases that work for you if these don't quite fit.)

g. Take a moment to imagine yourself free from this burden. What would you be like without this resentment or hurt? Jot down this vision and let it sink in.

h. End the practice by taking a few deep breaths and summoning some gratitude for this new possibility of release.

2. Self-Forgiveness Practice: "I Did the Best I Could with What I Had."
Once we begin to uncover, work with, and name our Inner Critics, a sense of anger or grief can come up. It is painful to see how much time and energy we have wasted listening to these voices. Instead of blaming ourselves, which continues to give power to the Inner Critic, we can practice self-forgiveness. Choosing self-forgiveness sets our hearts and minds on a new track, opening the possibility of freedom. Go through the above steps for forgiving others, changing the phrases so that they apply to yourself. (In the first step, the list is about all the resentments or insecurities you have about your flaws or mistakes.)

Be patient with yourself, and return to these exercises often. As resentments continue to surface, don't blame yourself. Be gentle. These exercises are not about *striving* or *forcing* yourself to forgive. The Wisdom inside you will help you fully let go when the timing is right. Your only job is to remain aware and accepting, and to keep showing up for yourself with love.

CHAPTER 9:
Granny Divine

*Never stand up when you can sit down,
and never sit down when you can lie down.*
—Winston S. Churchill

One day, I woke up with every intention to sit on the porch and write all morning. It was a lovely summer day, and life was good. I set up my laptop, made a cup of green tea, laid out my outline, and sat down to write.

"Hi, Chancho-boo-boo!" I said as my dog peeked his head into the porch. "Do you want to sit out here with me? Let me go get your bed and some toys."

Chancho wagged his tail and looked hopeful. He's my little shadow, comforted by being in the same room as me at all times. *Maybe I'll prop the door open so that he can come in and out of the front yard as he pleases*, I thought.

He grabbed his stuffed turtle, looked at me mischievously, and ran into the yard, inviting me to play. How could I deny him and crush his precious puppy spirit?

"Okay, just for a few minutes, Chanch," I said, following him into the sunshine.

He juked me, running around in circles, loving life. I couldn't help but laugh. He makes my heart sing.

"Watch out! I'm gonna getcha!" I taunted, jumping back and forth. A tug o' war ensued.

Suddenly, I noticed the weeds growing out of control in the flower bed. Before I knew it, I was on my hands and knees, pulling clovers and dandelions out of the wood chips. *I'll just do this for a few minutes*, I thought. *Just this one little section.* It felt so good to get my fingers in the soil. There's something healing about digging in the dirt that always makes my mind go blank. That day, I was getting in the flow, so I moved on to the next flower bed. Pretty soon, I'd taken up the shovel and started digging a new section so that I could transplant those hostas I'd been meaning to move for months. *This is super important*, I told myself. *I'm not procrastinating. I'm getting to things that have long been neglected.*

After half an hour, I was thirsty, so I headed inside for something cool to drink. My tea had cooled to room temperature, so I transferred it to a glass and added a few ice cubes. *Perfect. Ahhh.*

I was feeling a bit hungry then too. *You know what would go nicely with this tea? Some yogurt and blueberries! I'll just sit on the couch and eat it while I'm watching* The Daily Show *until my sweat dries, then I'll go back to writing.*

By that point, it was too late. I'd entered YouTube Land, and one thing led to the next as I was sucked into the black hole of the Internet. My intentions of meeting that day's goals could now wait until tomorrow. Keanu Reeves was playing with puppies while answering fan questions on BuzzFeed, and this could not be missed.

Enter Granny Divine.

You really deserve to rest, you know, she cooed in my head. *Your back is sore from all that gardening. Take a load off.* Her siren call seems irresistible. So alluring, so comforting. How could she possibly be an Inner Demon?

It wasn't until I suddenly looked at the time two hours later that I snapped out of her spell and berated myself for a whole morning lost. How many profiles of adoptable dogs had I read? How many TED Talks had I watched back to back? Why had I played that bit of Trevor Noah's stand-up for the fifth time? I had no idea. In horror, I saw the once-full Tupperware of cookies lying empty next to me on the couch. I realized I'd just had a procrastination blackout. Panic set in, followed by defeat and despair. *I may as well not even try*, I thought. *I'm a total failure. Maybe tomorrow I'll get my act together.* But for that moment, I headed back out to the garden as a way to lick my wounds and feel productive. At least my body would be moving and accomplishing something.

GRANNY DIVINE

This Inner Critic is so unlike the others. She seems so sweet, so well-intentioned. Wouldn't it be glorious to just lie my head on her bosom and drift off into a blissful state of disconnection and numbness? She just wants me to feel comfortable and happy—or so she convinces me.

Here, we must remember that not all sweet voices in our head are actually Inner Advocates. Just because she sounds nice doesn't mean she wants the best for us. This Inner Critic's role is to prevent us from growing into higher consciousness: to keep us from spiritual, psychological, and emotional evolution. It doesn't want us to expand outside of our well-worn ego patterns and into the unknown. Trying something new and risky threatens the ego's sense of self. Because our ego is who we mistake ourselves to be, whenever we step outside the box of our habituated personality to reach for transformation, the Inner Critic will be waiting for us—often with comfy pillows, warm tea, a crocheted lap blanket, and a good old-timey picture show.

Doing something new and good for us carries a threat. The apparent stability and predictability of the way things are *now*—the way things have always been—is at stake. So the ego jumps in and tries to protect us from potentially dangerous change by wooing us into shutdown mode. We dissociate from our bodies, lose energy, get brain fog, and can't stop yawning and daydreaming about a nap. We feel bored and can't focus. All these reactions are dear Granny Divine's way of saying, *Never change, dear. I love you just the way you are.* On the surface, that is a sweet message to tell ourselves. But it's also true that we all contain within us an infinite potential to learn and grow. While it is a helpful and necessary practice to accept ourselves just as we are, we also owe it to ourselves, our community, and the world to become the best possible version of ourselves. To use and develop our gifts and talents. To be of service.

For many people, whenever we try to do something good for ourselves, be it developing a new spiritual practice, starting a new hygiene routine, learning to create a spreadsheet, getting back into the dating scene, or addressing conflict, Granny Divine keeps getting in the way. The most recurrent example of this for me is when my dad is blabbering to me again about how to save and invest my money, and I can't absorb and retain the information. I instantly zone out, finding the La-Z-Boy recliner in my mind. I think about other things and just wait for him to finish his lecture. Another example is when my friends encourage me to apply to that awesome job; and when the time comes, my mind becomes lazy and sloppy. I forget to do it. Then I "forget" again the next day, and the next, until it's too late. Of course, I'm not actually forgetting. I'm just putting it off. *You can do that later*, Granny croons.

Some days, as soon as I sit down on a meditation cushion, I drift off to sleep. I'd had plenty of rest and was my spunky self two minutes prior, and yet I suddenly cannot resist the urge to slide off into dreamland. A sloth-like torpor overtakes my mind and body, and I give in to its lullaby. This same reaction often kicks in when I'm trying to listen to something I know I need to understand, something that will certainly improve my life (like a talk on the Inner Critic, the ego, nonduality, or non-self). *Snore!*

With meditation (and life in general), I tend to be an agitated and restless type instead of a slothy type. But last summer, after months of zoning out as soon as my butt hit the meditation cushion, I went to my teacher Mark in desperation. Was I losing all the momentum I had gained from years of practice? What was wrong with me?

As I explained my predicament to Mark, he gently smiled. "Congratulations! You're making progress," he said. "Your mind has learned a new trick! It has finally learned to relax. Now it's your job to get curious about the sleepiness. Be ready for it before you sit down, and notice it as soon as it shows up. You don't even need to fight it. Just be alert enough to watch what it feels like and to question why it is so alluring."

This tactic can apply to other areas of our lives as well, not just our spiritual practices. We can make note of which activities we tend to put off, forget about, or get a mushy mind about. Then we can be ready to observe our sloth before we enter into those situations. Expect it to show up, and make a commitment to get curious about it. Curiosity will keep your mind and body awake. Curiosity has a loving quality to it. It says, *I care enough about your life to pay attention and to experiment with something new.*

Granny Divine, that Inner Procrastinator, doesn't just distract us from our to-do list. She's also great at convincing us to avoid conflict, because conflict is uncomfortable. After all, what kind of evil grandma would want her grandchild to experience discomfort? This comes up for me whenever I feel a need to make amends for a hurtful action I've committed. I try to talk myself out of an apology, thinking that it will be awkward for the other person or hurt them more to talk about painful memories. Or that maybe they've forgotten about it already, and I should too.

Don't dredge up the past, dear, Granny Divine says every time. *I'll just sweep that under the rug for you.*

The truth is, my rug was starting to show bulges I could no longer ignore. I kept tripping on them, then walking away without pulling out the dustpan. My conscience needed a good cleaning. Why did I keep avoiding it? I was getting more and more agitated. In some cases, a friend or family member was doing something hurtful to me. Certainly, they were oblivious, so I figured I had no right to speak up. They weren't intentionally hurting me, so I thought I should just let it slide, even though we were steadily growing apart. The connection we once had was fading. Perhaps we were meant to grow apart. Oh well. Nothing I could do about it.

Don't rock the boat, dear, Granny Divine would say. *Just be nice.*

Just. Be. *Nice.*

Granny Divine's Lullaby versus Self-Care

The Inner Critic shows up in such sneaky ways. Oftentimes there is only a sliver of a difference between Granny Divine's voice and the voice of my compassionate Inner Advocate who is trying to prioritize my self-care. After all, I drive myself so hard most of the time that I need reminders to slow down and take a break. Sometimes Keanu Reeves playing with puppies is the exact medicine I need to give my mind and body a rest. So how to tell the difference between the justification of the Inner Procrastinator and the sound advice of Self-Love?

The skill that needs to be cultivated here is *discernment.* To differentiate between Wisdom and Delusion is no easy task, and it takes practice. We must remain interested in the reverberations in our heart that linger after we have made certain choices. Unfortunately, there is no rule book to be followed. It is a process of trial and error, of paying attention and learning from our mistakes. Sometimes I feel terrible after spending a few mindless hours on Netflix; other times, I feel filled up and rejuvenated. This demonstrates that there is not anything inherently wrong with certain activities. Instead, it is our motivations that matter.

Of course, as with anything, mindfulness helps our discernment when looking at intentions. If we're running on autopilot and neglecting our prayer and/or meditation practices, our mind will not be skilled enough to catch us in the act of self-sabotage. Such was the case with the procrastination story I shared to open this chapter. I didn't intentionally sit down to listen to my Inner Guidance—to get still, to let go, to breathe deeply—for about five days. In that short amount of time, my monkey mind had gained quite a bit of momentum.

By contrast, when I am clearing my mind daily and feeling the sensations in my body while sitting on the meditation cushion or in my "prayer chair," Wisdom naturally arises, and I can slow down enough to drop in some investigative questions. The exercises at the end of this chapter pose a few questions I've worked with and how they've helped me.

Remember, we all have an Inner Teenager who doesn't want to do the chores, finish the homework, or talk with that friend who made us angry. This rebellious teen just wants to sleep thirteen hours a day, skip class, and play video games. And they want to do all this at Grandma's house, not Mom's. This is normal, so don't beat yourself up for these desires. Luckily, in addition to this Inner Rebel, we all have an Inner Adult who knows what's best for us, who knows how to lovingly parent those compulsive urges with logical thinking, discipline, and boundaries. We need to get to know and trust this Inner Adult. Only then can we turn down Granny Divine's folly and listen to some *real* grandmotherly wisdom: to do something today that your future self will thank you for. Stay the course.

Since it was time to let Granny Divine know I'm all grown up now, I wrote her this letter:

BLESSING MY DEMONS

Dear Granny Divine,

I'm writing today to say THANK YOU for all your sweet gifts. It wasn't even my birthday, and you still showered me with glucose, carbohydrates, mind-numbing entertainment, and escape routes from my responsibilities. How kind of you! And that "Get Out of Discomfort for Free Card!" was such a creative present!

I really want to repay you for your well-intentioned gestures, so I've come up with a plan. Each time you try to give me one of your gifts, I will give you one in return. Your gift is a reminder and reassurance that I am an adult now and that I can make my own decisions about comfort, conflict, hard work, self-care, and discipline. Rest assured that you needn't worry about me.

So go. Enjoy your retirement to its fullest. Bring treats to your friends at the bridge tournament, indulge in Wheel of Fortune, *and take a long nap. There will be times when I will still want and need to hang out with you and show you all my favorite YouTube videos. When I am driving myself too harshly, forgetting to be kind to myself, or truly neglecting my rest and self-care, please let me know. Just stop distracting me from the difficult things that are actually good for me, please and thank you.*

With love,
Your adult granddaughter, Chelsea

YOUR TURN!
Inner Work Exercises

When you feel the urge to get offtrack, indulge your Inner Teenager, and listen to Granny Divine instead of getting to that thing that is good for you, follow these steps:

1. Stop, Take Three Deep Breaths, and Ask Yourself, "How Will I Feel After Doing This? Better? Or Worse?"
For any investigation to be honest, we first need to pause, breathe, and connect with our body. Even two or three conscious breaths shift the energy. I know I have gathered enough "data" from my life to answer the question above honestly when I can remember to ask it. I have made enough choices and have been paying attention to their effects closely enough that I can usually tell when an urge to do something will leave me satisfied or feeling crummy about myself afterward. If I can't quite tell, I ask the next question.

2. Ask Yourself, "Am I Experiencing Any Resistance? Or Running from Something? What Am I Avoiding, and Why?"
For me, when I'm in the throes of procrastination momentum, my mind is too wily and moving too fast to parse out any deeper truth by just thinking about these questions. What works for me is taking five to ten minutes to write about it. Writing forces me to slow my mind down into a comprehensible sequence, and I can tease out the stories I'm telling myself and the real feelings I'm running from.

3. Ask Yourself, "Is This Procrastination Keeping Me from Taking Risks That Are Good for Me?" Employ Your Higher Self or Inner Adult to Answer This Question.

Usually, the answer is a big fat yes. For me, procrastination tends to cover my fear of success, of getting "too big for my britches." Following fear over love is certainly not a value of mine, and yet I do it again and again. Fear can be so convincing, making me believe that vulnerability is a horrible idea when my experience and my Higher Self know that risking vulnerability is the only path toward freedom. By "Higher Self," I mean that grounded and wise part of us that resides in the center of our Being. Some call it our True Self, our Essence, our Soul, our Inner Divinity, our Pure Consciousness, or our Big Mind. We all have access to it, no matter how unpracticed and neurotic we may be. Even if you don't believe in such silly things, you can still tap into it.

Don't believe me? That's fine. But check it out for yourself—and come up with your own word for it.

PS: Don't pretend to justify laziness by insisting that Winston Churchill endorsed it. (See the epigraph at the beginning of this chapter.) Obviously, he was such a busy and accomplished person. Maybe he did his work while lying down to conserve energy to be more productive. . . . Or perhaps he was truly fighting his Inner Couch Potato, just like the rest of us.

CHAPTER 10:
The Boss of Bludgeon

On every level of life, from housework to heights of prayer, in all judgment and efforts to get things done, hurry and impatience are sure marks of the amateur.
—Evelyn Underhill

"Pleasure? Huh. What is it good for? Absolutely nothing!"

This has been my motto for much of my adult life. Not consciously, of course. There is some story in me that convinces me the righteous path is the exhausting one—the one that will have me slogging through mud, never resting, never stopping to smell the flowers. Clearly, God's will for me is to sell all my belongings, leave everything behind, and move across the world to help disadvantaged and diseased children by staring lovingly into their eyes as they each breathe their last breath. Or become a nun who shaves her head, lives in a cave, and sits on a rock, meditating for eighteen hours a day in ascetic isolation. Or spend the rest of my life in prison as a conscientious objector, writing poems and manifestos on social reform and liberation, inspiring the masses to wake up and create sweeping political, economic, and spiritual changes. Doing anything less is lazy and selfish, right?

Worthless piece of scum that I am, I have yet to accomplish any of these goals. And yet I'm usually busy, running around like a chicken with my head cut off so that I can assure my Inner Critic that I'm working on it. One glimpse at my calendar would make anyone have a near-panic attack. It is often scheduled out to the very last minute. When I do have a moment to spare, sometimes I naturally sit down because my body needs a rest. The self-flagellation creeps in soon afterward: *All right. Your minute's up, you slob! Back to work! Look at these floors! And those books shoved onto the shelf in such haphazard order!* Just like that, I find myself frantically sweeping, vacuuming, returning emails, or alphabetizing books. Sure, I'm not competing with Mother Teresa with these antics, but at least my house is ready for guests at any moment. As they say, "Cleanliness is next to Godliness," and my Inner Critic allows for that to be good enough. Until I stop to rest, that is. Then it's back at me, whipping me from behind with an itching, restless feeling of anxiety.

The word *taskmaster* doesn't even come close to the inner pressure to "do more, do better, do faster, or else!" This particular version of my Inner Critic has had me trapped in servitude my whole life. As long as I'm working, it leaves me alone. Stopping to rest is not worth dealing with all the feelings of inadequacy and worthlessness that barrage me when I try to take a nap, watch a mindless romantic comedy, lie outside in the sun, or read a novel. The pleasure of these activities does not outweigh the inner lashings I must endure both during and afterward.

When I was a kid, I loved the Lord of the Rings franchise. I was introduced to it through the animated films from the late '70s and early '80s. *The Return of the King* featured a scene that seared itself into my memory, and with good reason. The heroes of the story, Frodo and Samwise, are attempting to sneak through the evil territory of Mordor in disguise, wearing the armor of their enemies. They are taken in by an army of Orcs, who mistake them for little Orcs. The leader of the battalion menacingly cracks his whip behind the backs of the terrified Hobbits and the exhausted Orcs while they are forced to march on endlessly, singing battle songs like "Where There's a Whip (There's a Way)" to keep their feet moving at a steady tempo.

Of course, this scene imprinted itself on my preteen mind because that song gave me a taste of what was to become the underlying background music of my life. (Plus, the song is catchy.) I had an inner Orc overlord, and his name was the Boss of Bludgeon. He was sneaking his way into my consciousness, always whipping me from behind to do more.

THE BOSS OF BLUDGEON

BLESSING MY DEMONS

The daily slog set in. First, accomplish all your work, *then* reward yourself with rest and play. The problem was that the checklist was never complete, so rest and play felt like a criminal indulgence, sneaking away from the Master, going AWOL. If I did manage to convince myself to break ranks for a few moments of blessed relief, I had to march twice as fast to get caught back up. The hedonism of leisure could not be tolerated.

Case in point: my Netflix queue. It is filled with documentaries about wars, genocide, climate change, feminist history, and explanations of the machinations of racism. Who would ever want to watch that depressing shit with me on a Friday night? But if I'm going to spend two whole hours sitting still and eating junk food, I better damn well *earn* it by learning something of substance and value. (*Study the truth, Chelsea. Not silly fantasies of romantic nonsense—which would further brainwash you through Disney's heteronormative narratives—or the foolishness of sci-fi conspiracy theory!*)

Also, take the current stack of books I'm reading as another example of the Boss of Bludgeon's influence. There's some LGBTQ history mixed in with a whole lot of spiritual self-help books and theology, followed by something related to career development. God forbid I would ever allow myself to read a novel! Every summer I tell myself, "This is it. This summer, I'm going to read at least two novels from my shelf just for the pure joy of it!" Rarely does this happen. When I was a teenager, I voraciously read fantasy novels with no remorse. Where has that child gone? I want her back. The capability to rest in pleasure for pleasure's sake has all but left me. Somewhere along the way, I began to value being a serious, busy, productive, joyless adult. Bummer.

For the longest time, I could never sit still enough to answer this question honestly. With years of incremental practice of contemplative prayer and mindful meditation, I've built up a tolerance for stillness. In that stillness, I discovered my feelings. I noticed that when my emotions reared their head, there arose in me a strong desire to get up and run back to my to-do list. After watching this pattern for a while, I realized that all my frenetic do-gooder activity was a way to avoid feeling my feelings. When I was accomplishing things and my body had a task, I didn't need to be with my grief, my shame, or my anger. In the beginning, doing this alone was too hard. However, sitting in a room of other meditators applied the appropriate amount of pressure to stay on the cushion. Peer pressure has its place.

The flurry of activity (especially around organizing and cleaning things) and committing oneself to admirable causes is exaggerated in **Enneagram Ones** (like me). It's our particular way of placating the Inner Critic and avoiding the difficult emotions and thoughts that arise with stillness. You may think I'm overly obsessive about being a clean freak (I'm not saying I'm not), but other Enneagram types have their own version of avoiding their feelings. Let's take a look.

Enneagram Twos repress their feelings by taking on the feelings and needs of others. Their compulsive activity tends to be around sending birthday cards, meeting with friends to maintain connections, and planning events that will enrich and nurture others, usually at their own expense. While Twos are constantly feeling everyone else's feelings, it is incredibly difficult for them to feel and name their own emotions and needs.

Enneagram Threes avoid their feelings by overworking, creating elaborate checklists, accomplishing their many goals, obsessing over efficiency, and being successful and outstanding. Emotions are messy, and they get in the way of that process of efficiency. So Threes learn to bypass their feelings, instead focusing on what other people need them to be and setting about to accomplish that.

Enneagram Fours are tossed about by their emotional highs and lows, so they employ a brilliant tactic in getting around this: they learn to "curate moods." Fours will find themselves feeding a certain emotion to keep it going for hours, days, or even weeks. They accomplish this through many creative strategies, such as listening to melancholic music, digging up old letters from past lovers, or comparing themselves to people who are "doing better at life" than they are. These moods are contrived, and the full range of authentic emotions remains elusive.

Enneagram Fives detach from their feelings by studying them from an intellectual vantage point. They *think* their feelings instead of feeling them. They also tend to avoid the messiness of life by isolating themselves and cramming in and retaining as much information in their brains as possible. They get lost down the rabbit hole of research, so to speak. No room to feel the heart or the body when the mechanisms of the mind are on overdrive.

Enneagram Sixes experience a lot of anxiety, as well as a slew of other emotions. To escape this, they begin planning, worrying, doubting, and strategizing about how to avoid disaster. All of their circular contingency planning tricks them into believing they are working on their problems and gives them a sense of security. In reality, thinking about stressful things creates more stress. It is a trap. Their self-doubt and insistence on playing devil's advocate can keep them from taking meaningful action.

Enneagram Sevens are masters of avoiding difficult feelings. They accomplish this by constantly anticipating the next exciting adventure, whether that be a new project, an exotic vacation, or a potential new lover. They have an uncanny capability to reframe any negative experience into a positive one. While this optimism is admirable on some accounts, Sevens don't allow themselves to process through and heal their old wounds—because that is a painful process, and they'd rather just stay happy and stimulated. They may dip into grief, anger, jealousy, or shame from time to time, but they just as quickly dip out, as their tolerance for painful emotions is so low.

Enneagram Eights avoid their full range of emotions by making themselves invulnerable to fear. They learned that vulnerability must be avoided at all costs, so they develop a tough skin as armor against threats. No tears or fears here, thank you very much! Just strength and power. Eights tend to get busy overworking themselves and affecting change with intensity and passion. They don't realize that intensity is not an emotion. It is a bodily energetic state. In fact, when Eights first start noticing feelings, they experience them almost exclusively as bodily sensations.

Enneagram Nines have no problem dodging their feelings. When difficulties arise, either within or without, they withdraw into their "happy place." In this inner sanctuary, Nines can relive good memories, imagine being on a gorgeous mountaintop, or generally self-soothe by chatting with a ruminating inner dialogue. Nines can numb out through food, books, television, endless Internet scrolling, or even exercise. While physically present with others in a room, they are often mentally "out to lunch."

Regardless of our personality type, most Westerners don't have an extensive emotional vocabulary. We know the categories of *sad, angry, happy,* and *afraid*. That's about it. Most of us are not taught to explore the many shades of sadness, including depression, despair, heavyheartedness, grief, disappointment, or melancholy. When we only have the word *sad*, we don't get very far in understanding ourselves or the roots of our feelings.

My friend Ryan, a psychotherapist, introduced me to using feeling wheels and feeling lists. He is obsessed with using them. He carries one in his pocket at all times, which is an admirable quirk. We could all benefit from pulling out a list several times a day to check in with our true emotions and build this vocabulary. When we're feeling unsettled, ambiguously agitated, or just "off," sometimes just naming the true feeling helps cool it down. In taking a look at a feelings list, I can look up the general category of *tense* and discover the many different flavors of that feeling, including *cranky, distraught, fidgety, nervous, overwhelmed,* and *restless*. Once I can be more specific about what I'm feeling, then what?

There is a story from Buddhist folklore that will be instructive here. On the night of his enlightenment, while sitting under the Bodhi Tree, the Buddha is met with a barrage of torments and temptations from the demon Mara. The archetypal figure Mara represents self-doubt, fear, greed, delusion, judgment, lust, or any other internal state that distracts us from being free. As the Buddha is approaching enlightenment, the demon shows up and tries to distract the diligent meditator by showing him visions of beautiful women. But the Buddha just smiles at him and says, "I see you, Mara," and Mara flees. Later, the demon returns with a new plan and begins hurtling flames and monsters at the Buddha to scare him off. But the Buddha is not confused. "I see you, Mara," he says again.

Finally, the demon returns with his most insidious trick. He tries to get the Buddha to doubt that he is worthy of achieving freedom and happiness. Mara mocks him, saying, "No mortal human can achieve this! Enlightenment belongs to *me!*" Then Mara demands that the Buddha call forth witnesses to prove his worthiness (like the Imposter Police!). "Who will speak for you?" he sneers. The Buddha simply touches the earth beneath him for support, and the Earth cries out, "I bear you witness!" Terrified and out of tricks, Mara disappears.

Once I'm clear about what I'm feeling, I can say, "I see you, restlessness." Just like Mara trying to sneak up on the Buddha, our emotions creep in and try to take the wheel. And just like the Buddha, we can say, "I see you, anxiety. You can ride along with Mara, but only in the passenger seat. I am driving." There is an alert and detached Presence available that is not afraid of the difficult emotions that come and go.

We can learn several things from this story about the Buddha and Mara. Certainly, beating ourselves up over our emotions doesn't work. If we do that, Mara wins. The harder we drive ourselves, the more fixated we become. For me, as an Enneagram One whose ego strategy is to turn myself into a self-improvement project, I cannot cure that part of myself by striving to be better about it. That would be working on ego *with* ego! We cannot adjust our patterned minds by approaching them through the same pattern. This is true for every Enneagram type.

So what is the alternative? Compassion! (Have you caught on to the pattern by now?)

There is not one personality type who instinctively uses compassion as a means of emotional avoidance. Therefore, compassion is always appropriate. The word itself breaks down into *com* ("being with") and *passion* ("suffering"). Thus, *compassion* means "being with suffering," allowing ourselves to get close to it with an open heart, without fear. We see this in children who want to bury a dead bird. Their hearts are broken; and yet with determination and gentleness, they dig that grave and say a prayer for the bird's happiness on the other side. We see this compassion in a daughter who has the presence to sit with her dying parent and be with the questions, fears, and pain, both those of her parent and her own. Compassion shows up when someone is going through a divorce with an alcoholic spouse and can see the alcoholic as a suffering human being who did their best despite the chaos that ensued.

Compassion requires fierce courage. It is far from wimpy. It inherently involves qualities of curiosity and interest in the other, and it resists the urge to run for the hills. Compassion allows us to breathe through the pain—whether ours or someone else's—until it transmutes into a bittersweet gift. And strangely, it has the power to affect change, both big and small.

There have been many points in my life when I've set the goal to daily floss my teeth, usually every six months after being embarrassed by the dentist, who says, "That's a lot of blood. You've got to start flossing." Every time I tried, I could never keep it up. My self-discipline persistently eluded me on this issue. So one day, I got out a dry-erase marker and wrote on my bathroom mirror, *FLOSS, YOU IDIOT!!!*

I thought it was the perfect solution to my dilemma: a daily reminder—and a daily lashing if I failed to follow through. Surely, if I really cracked down on myself, I could do it this time around. I flossed for two days, then quit again. What the heck was wrong with me?

I mentioned this conundrum to my Twelve Step sponsor in an offhand way one day. "What a cruel way to motivate yourself!" she exclaimed. "Perhaps you could try switching to using this phrase: 'Just for today, I will floss my teeth.'" So I erased the words of the Boss of Bludgeon and replaced them with these kinder words of encouragement.

I have barely missed a day of flossing in the four years since. Turns out kindness and gentleness actually work.

At an Inner Critic workshop with Enneagram educators Michael Naylor and Lynda Roberts in 2018, my cohorts and I were led through a simple visualization exercise that has changed my life and my relationship with my Inner Critic, particularly with the Boss of Bludgeon. First, Michael and Lynda had us envision our Inner Critic to get a clear image of what it looked like and felt like when it was harassing us. (For some people, their image was a tornado, a giant hammer, or a noxious gas. So far, all my images have turned out to be actual characters, most of them humanlike.) I brought to mind that Orc with his bludgeon in hand, but I couldn't see him clearly since he was always whipping me from behind. My experience of him was always a feeling of being pushed to stay in motion, accompanied by the background noise of anxiety.

Next, Michael and Lynda asked us to move our Inner Critic away from us in our mind's eye and notice any changes. Intuitively, I brought the sadistic Orc around to the front of me, where I could get a good look at him. To my amazement, I discovered that he was tiny, about the size of a five-year-old. I quickly snatched the weapon from his hand before he could use it again. Suddenly, in his ensuing tantrum, I noticed how cute he was. Without his whip and club, he was powerless. I patted him on the head and bent down to kiss his forehead. Like a street dog hungry for love, he melted at the gentle touch.

These days, when I am meditating on my cushion, or reading a book just for the fun of it (yes, I've learned to do this—at least occasionally), my Orc friend still comes to visit me and begins whipping me and prodding me from behind. Instead of jumping to my feet in a furor of productivity, I close my eyes, reach behind me, and pull Mr. Bludgeon into my lap. He has now shrunk to the size of a feral cat, and I soothe him by rubbing his back and tired shoulders with love. It's a lot of work to be constantly cracking a whip—and even Mordor's hellions, like me, need some good ol'-fashioned R&R now and then. Sometimes it takes several minutes of deep breathing to lure my little friend off to sleep. As he drifts away into dreamland, I smile and get back to my book.

This changed relationship with the Boss of Bludgeon has taken work and intention on my part. It all started with writing him this love note:

Dear Mr. Bludgeon,

You've got a rough job, commanding a battalion of warrior Orcs. You've gotta have some thick armor and thick skin. I can't even imagine how exhausted you are, marching miles on end each day, cracking that heavy whip over your head repeatedly, your voice hoarse from shouting orders over the din of clanging weapons and Orc-ish squabbles.

What a nightmare. Your poor feet and swollen ankles! As the one always in control and responsible for productivity rates, you must miss the spontaneity of shooting the shit around the fire with your buddies, playing games that aren't training drills, and taking a good old-fashioned nap. I feel so bad that you're under constant pressure from your Master to keep up the pace. Truly, you don't deserve this treatment.

What you deserve is some R&R. Better yet, a professional massage, some acupuncture, and a safe space to talk about your feelings. It would bring me great joy to see you cut yourself some slack, to stop and smell the lilacs.

Put down the club and the whip, take some deep breaths, and leave the endless war behind. Leave someone else to fight the battle of efficiency and productivity, because it's a fight that cannot be won. There's always more to do, more kingdoms to be conquered. Being busy and in charge does not define your worth. Tell your Master, the Dark Lord, that he can shove this whip where the sun don't shine, because you're not going to be his slave any longer!

In slothful solidarity, with potato chip crumbs on her shirt,
Chelsea

YOUR TURN!
Inner Work Exercises

1. Memorize the Acronym HALT

This is a tool used in some Twelve Step groups. It stands for "hungry, angry, lonely, and tired." Whenever you notice one of these states creeping up on you, give yourself permission to stop and address it. If you're hungry, eat before you get cranky and say something you regret. If you're angry, punch a pillow, go for a run, or write a stream-of-consciousness rant. Then go talk to a trusted friend or mentor to sort it out.

If you are lonely, do not isolate yourself. Reach out and go out. Texting doesn't count. To stave off loneliness, we need to be with real people in person—or at least hear their voice. If the first friend you call is not available, keep calling until you find someone who is. A good laugh or cry with a dear friend can vanquish loneliness in a heartbeat.

Lastly, if you are tired, take a nap. Prioritize getting eight hours of sleep each night. Adequate sleep is proven to address a whole slew of physical, mental, and emotional issues. Prioritize your self-care today. Your Inner Critic may have some opinions about that, but they are only foolish opinions. You deserve health and happiness, and you are the only one who can administer that. All of this may seem in direct contradiction to what we just learned about Granny Divine. But remember, the key here is *balance* between doing and resting. True self-care involves a healthy measure of both.

2. Go Online and Find a Feelings Wheel or Feelings Chart That You Like

Print it out and keep it where you will see it. You can even print a mini version, laminate it, and keep it in your wallet. Check in with the list at least once a day to find where you are currently residing or which feelings you have journeyed through that day. Make sure to check in with how this emotion feels *in your body*. Experiencing emotions as energy and sensations will help you become more proficient at identifying them. If you feel inspired, you can journal about it each night to further solidify your friendship with yourself!

3. Try Michael and Lynda's Inner Critic Visualization

    a. Close your eyes and bring to mind a time when your Inner Critic was on your case. Envision what this entity looks like. There are no limits or rules. Whatever comes to mind is the correct image for you.

    b. Move this Inner Critic away from you. Again, anything goes (as long as it's not cruel!). Let your imagination run wild, and do not try to control it. Notice how the feeling or relationship changes when the Inner Critic is not so close. Is there any action you or the Inner Critic take when you're not in such close proximity?

    c. Notice the tension or stress present in the Inner Critic character. What words of kindness, advice, or well wishes can you offer to your Inner Critic?

    d. When you feel like you're done with the visualization, draw a quick sketch of your image of the Inner Critic, and write it a letter of Blessing.

    e. Notice the emotional and psychological impact this exercise has had on you. Jot down a note about that as well.

CHAPTER 11:
Thoressa

My religion is based on truth and non-violence. Truth is my God. Non-violence is the means of realizing Him.
—Mahatma Gandhi

This chapter may seem like it's off-subject. But just hang with me and be patient. It will connect back.

One time, I was walking with a tour group down Shuhada Street in Hebron, in the West Bank of Palestine. The sun was beating down on my head, and my water bottle was already empty. It was August 2015. Here, within a mile of the burial grounds of Father Abraham (yes, *the* Father Abraham), the former shops in the once-bustling Palestinian marketplace were boarded up, since families and businesses had been forced to leave their cultural and economic center. Israelis roamed the streets freely, while it was illegal for native Palestinians to walk there.

"If a Palestinian wants to get to that side of the street," our tour guide Alon explained, "they must walk around about a mile on the streets that are designated for them. Soldiers will harass and arrest them if they walk here. What you are witnessing is two separate sets of laws within one country: apartheid."

Oh my God, was my reaction. *I thought apartheid had been eradicated once and for all in South Africa. How did I not know about this?*

Alon was a former Israeli soldier. He explained how the first Palestinian he'd ever met had eerily reminded him of his grandmother. She was an old woman whose home he had blown a hole in with explosives before chasing out the whole family at gunpoint and turning their house into a "military outpost." These operations are called "straw widows" and are a common way to evict Palestinian civilians from their homes, all in the name of military training. Alon was now working for Breaking the Silence, an organization of ex-military personnel who give testimony to the human rights violations they committed while serving in the Israeli military. He was haunted every night by his crimes, and he found his current work to be the only way to atone for his sins.

As we continued walking, Alon went on to explain the cages we were seeing around the balconies and windows above us. They were there to protect Palestinian families from attacks by Israeli settlers, who frequently threw stones, garbage, and even feces at them as they went about their lives. The attacks on Palestinian children as they walked to school were so severe that international peacekeepers had to walk with them on their daily route to keep them safe.

Suddenly, five Israeli soldiers touting machine guns ran around the corner of a shop, shouting in Hebrew.

"Don't worry," Alon said. "They're just running a drill. They have declared this as a 'military training zone' and they run these drills frequently—oftentimes on Palestinians who have no warning and are not told it is a drill."

"Go, go, go!" the soldiers shouted in English, now apparently performing for us. Some posted up to cover the others, who kicked in a shop door to clear the building. My heart was racing despite my knowing it was only practice. I wasn't used to men with loaded machine guns on every street corner. But this was the norm here, a way of life that had been ongoing for the last seventy years.

After all the unfolding drama in the streets of Hebron, visiting the Tomb of the Patriarchs was horribly underwhelming. Father Abraham's grave was just a green box behind bars. I could still feel the violent reverberations from the massacre of 29 Muslims and the injury of 125 others who had been worshipping right in that spot, gunned down by Baruch Goldstein during Ramadan in 1994. (The Tomb of the Patriarchs is a holy site for Jews, Christians, and Muslims.) Goldstein was a physician who had been born in Brooklyn, New

York, and later immigrated to Israel and became a religious extremist. While the majority of Israelis have since denounced his actions and labeled him a terrorist, his gravesite remained, with an epitaph that read, "A martyr with clean hands and a pure heart." For a holy site that was supposed to be sacred, there was no feeling of mystical connection to my ancestors here. It reeked of fear, unspeakable grief, hatred, and trauma. Our tour group didn't stay long.

Back outside in the deserted streets, we encountered two Israeli soldiers—young men right out of high school, wearing their green combat gear and helmets as they approached us. I asked Alon how he could get away with openly slandering his government right in front of military personnel. "They can't do anything to me," he said, smirking wearily. "I'm Israeli."

He began a brief and friendly dialogue with the two young men then. One of them turned to us and, with bitterness in his voice, told us, "I don't want to be doing this. I'm twenty-one years old; and I want to be hanging out with my friends, drinking beer, and having a girlfriend. Instead, I'm stuck here, forced to hold a machine gun for three years. I hate it. It sucks." He had no choice in the matter. Military service was conscripted for all Israeli citizens.

I was visiting the Holy Land with a group called Peace Not Walls, and we were there to listen to the stories of Israelis and Palestinians about their experiences with the ongoing conflict in their homeland. Before this trip, I had always been so sure of my stance on everything, insisting that my views were correct—and getting furious at anyone who dared to present another opinion. Having surrounded myself with peace activists in college, I had heard snippets of the horrors Palestinians were going through and the international laws the Israeli government was continually breaking. In my mind, Israelis were the bad guys. All of them. Now, in the West Bank, my anger was turning into confusion.

Here, it's important to clarify the difference between Israelis and Jews. While all Israelis are Jews (it's required if you want to be a citizen of the country), not all Jews are Israeli. There are some Jews who believe that the land was given to them by God, and therefore everyone else must be forced off it. Many other Jews oppose modern Israel's land-grabbing politics and have turned away from the colonizing narrative, believing that Israel's land can be shared with the native Palestinians who live there. It is not anti-Semitic to oppose modern Israel's oppressive political tactics. To oppose these political tactics is anti-colonial and anti-apartheid.

As our days in Palestine and Israel rolled on, the group and I witnessed countless ongoing tragedies. Palestinian homes were demolished in the middle of the night by the Israeli government, displacing peaceful families who had lived there for generations. We went to a refugee camp that had a wall listing the names of over two hundred Palestinian children who had been murdered in a massacre in July 2014 by Israeli soldiers (with tanks and missiles supplied by the United States). A huge concrete wall about one hundred miles long that separates the Palestinian West Bank from Israel was covered in messages of hope and despair and topped with gun turret towers. We visited the Holocaust Museum in Jerusalem, where our tour guide was an old Jewish man whose parents had been tortured by Nazis. His family had needed refuge, and Israel had provided a safe place for the Jewish people after World War II. Illegal Israeli settlement communities with Olympic-sized swimming pools and public fountains dotted the Palestinian territories, right next to poor Palestinian homes whose water supply was only turned on once every couple of weeks.

We went to holy sites like Mount of Beatitudes, Bethlehem, and Golgotha, a hill where five thousand olive trees had been planted to commemorate the very spot where Jesus had fed the crowd with only five loaves and two fish. We also encountered military checkpoints, road blockades restricting freedom of movement, and graffiti honoring Palestinians who had fought back against their imprisonment and displacement, killing innocent Israeli citizens with grenades or rocket launchers.

On our last day at the Mount of Olives, our group of fifteen young Americans was sitting in a room with an Israeli woman named Raya and a young Palestinian woman named Ma'isha. This was the only time during the trip when we encountered an Israeli and a Palestinian together in the same room. Raya, in her late fifties, sat in a green cotton dress while recounting the story of her husband's murder by a Palestinian. Halfway through, Ma'isha reached out to hold Raya's hand, and I noticed they both had silent tears streaming down their faces. I felt like I hadn't exhaled since Raya's story had begun.

To my surprise, Raya finished her story by stating, "This small country is big enough for all of us to live here. Trust me. I have been arrested countless times in acts of civil disobedience in an attempt to stop my people from stealing Palestinian land. It's not right. They don't deserve this genocide." This woman seemed to be an angel, a goddess, a bodhisattva. How could she love her enemies after what they had stolen from her?

Ma'isha, who was wearing fashionable skinny jeans and a green blouse, took her turn next. Her voice was strained from the beginning. Her favorite brother had been shot in the street by an Israeli soldier, having committed no crime and without any trial. Her hands waved about forcefully as she told her story. I could see her toes clenching, her left leg rapidly bouncing as she talked. And yet she finished her story with this statement: "The Jews don't need to leave! The Jews need to live here. Raya needs a home too. We are neighbors. We need each other!"

These two brave women were breaking the norm of separation and hatred between two supposed enemy groups. Amid the chaos, they had become unlikely friends, traveling around the country and telling their stories with a group called the Parents Circle-Families Forum. There was not a dry eye among us as we witnessed their concluding embrace. They had found a way to step out of the cycles of hatred and see their enemies as suffering human beings, just like them. They had found a way to retain their dignity in a sea of undignified, unmitigated violence and misunderstanding.

In this room, as I witnessed the power of radical forgiveness, something inside me cracked. My whole identity of being the person who is right, the person who channeled her motivation and energy from her righteous anger, suddenly made no sense. This crack in my breaking heart allowed me to experience a sea of grief and confusion unlike any I had ever known. It was as if I were grieving and acknowledging the pain of the whole world, my whole life, and all the absurdity I had kept at a safe distance through rationalization, adamantly choosing sides, and pretending I had control over the outcomes.

This surrender to the pain allowed me to tap into the deep well of compassion covered up inside my hardened heart.

Suddenly, and with a clarity and assuredness I had never known, I knew that the only logical response to violence and ignorance is *love*. Anger, hatred, and blame no longer made any sense. We were *all* suffering. Even the sick child murderers. Even the greedy corporate bosses who lobby in favor of climate denial so that they can keep raping our planet. Even the white nationalists who rallied in Charlottesville, carrying Nazi flags in 2017. Even fascist political leaders who spout homophobic propaganda to stir up fear among their constituency. In their own way, each is suffering from their fear, isolation, and hatred.

While growing up in Minnesota, I constantly heard derogatory jokes about people from our neighboring state of Iowa. ("What does IOWA stand for? Idiots out wandering around! Ha ha ha!") Ironically, the southern half of Minnesota is just like Iowa, all corn and soybean fields. So most of the corny jokes could just as well apply to Minnesotans. Why our neighbors in North and South Dakota were never picked on, I'll never know. Wisconsinites got their fair share of jabs in jest, but that was mostly in good fun due to the football rivalry between the Packers and the Vikings.

This tendency to "other" groups of people or individuals is happening everywhere, all around us. To say people are "other" based on arbitrary state lines is only the beginning. We do this in ways that are both subtle and obvious:

- "We're Americans. They are Mexicans." (Um, almost half of the US used to be part of Mexico.)
- "I could never be friends with a Republican/Democrat!" (Really? I bet you already are.)
- "Stay away from that neighborhood. Those people are dangerous!" (*All* of them? Or just the small handful we've seen on the news?)
- "I'll never understand women!" (Listening to them would remedy that quickly.)

In my own life, I've watched myself unconsciously do this around religious beliefs. In high school, I othered atheists by writing them off as ignorant, out of touch, and (quite frankly) stupid. Then, in my young adult years, I easily flipped that script on to Evangelical Fundamentalists. Why does this dynamic happen so regularly, and in so many forms?

Part of it seems to be about safety, trust, and belonging. Humans have always been social creatures, first living in small groups and tribes, then in villages and cities. There was a sense of safety that was created by knowing the people in one's own group, taking care of one another, sharing resources, and developing bonds of trust and friendship. People outside of the group were to be looked upon with suspicion and caution. Knowing clearly who fit into the categories of "us" and "them" made life safer and less chaotic. It also provided a sense of identity and belonging, a strong sense of self.

Soon, humans began to define themselves based on who they were *not*. ("I am a Minnesotan, *not* a Wisconsinite.") Of course, this fairly innocent interstate sibling rivalry is nothing compared to the othering used by whole societies and governments to declare war, commit genocide, or lock people away in prisons with lifetime sentences. But all of these atrocious acts were (and still are) possible because most people are not examining their prejudices or getting to know people outside of their "tribe." We define our positive self-image by negating what we are not:

- "At least I'm not a savage. We are civilized."
- "They deserve it. They are criminals!"
- "Those heathens disgust me! God wants righteous people to rule this land!"
- "Your skin color makes me afraid! I guess I'll have to shoot you."

I contribute to creating this narrative and this toxic culture when I choose to not talk to certain family members due to their politics, or when I avoid certain neighbors because they are of a different culture or class. This distancing starts small, with one little choice at a time. But pretty soon, there is a chasm between us, and I can no longer feel their humanity. I have thrown them out of my heart. If they are struggling, in pain, or oppressed, I don't feel it because it feels like there is a wall between us. I am the one who built that wall, and I am the one who can take it down. This will take time, and it will take intention. Perhaps it starts with a hello and eye contact, then writing a letter or making a phone call. I will likely need to be the first one to make a move. If

I've been involved in creating an "other," even if only in my mind, I have some amends to make.

Who is this conquering tyrant within me who runs around, arbitrarily drawing boundaries and borders between my heart and others? She loves to march around and plant flags in the ground, claiming her right to speak over others, act against others, and dismiss others' viewpoints. There is a strange little part inside me that refuses to trust another's perspective. It wants only to listen to information that already confirms her worldview, and it enjoys gossiping about the suspicious and backward ways of those different from her. She wants to argue with the anonymous swarms of enemies on social media. She gets very defensive when her known territory is intruded upon by differing perspectives, lifestyles, beliefs, or politics. She draws a hard line in the sand and prepares to defend herself against the Other. She also hunkers down to steep herself in gratitude for being a part of the "enlightened" group.

I'll call her Thoressa, Defender of the Enlightened Few. She believes it feels great to be one of the "good guys." Part of the cool kids club. The political party God favors. The true believers. The rational, objective thinkers.

As good as it feels to be part of the imaginary "enlightened few," when I stopped to examine this view, it fell short of what it was trying to bring me, which was safety and belonging. Instead, she just made me feel paranoid, tight, and defensive. Thoressa needed a reassignment:

Dearest Thoressa,

You have been a fabulous Defender of the Enlightened Few for much of my life. You've diligently tried to make sure I have a solid place to stand in this world, surrounded by supportive and faithful comrades. These compatriots have brought a sense of safety because we know and understand their views. They are predictable; they follow the script.

Having an open and curious mind feels dangerous. And you've certainly advised me against an open and curious heart! To you, being open to listening to, understanding, and loving those on the "outside" seems foolish. You coached me that if my heart is open to everyone, then I will be adrift on moving sands, traversing everywhere and belonging nowhere and with no one. You've worked hard in defending me from this type of loneliness. Thank you.

Now that I'm older, I see a flaw in this battle tactic. Being limited to interact with and be close to only an Enlightened Few is what is causing the loneliness! My heart now has a deeper desire than belonging to a select club. It wants to belong to the whole human race! I've experienced that feeling now, and it's beautiful! It's a feeling of vast expansion, a feeling of freedom! The freedom to love everyone who crosses my path and to understand that their story connects me with different cultures, new ways of seeing, and new friends.

Our old tactic was one of creating enemies. We were surrounded by them on all sides. With this new strategy, we are actually increasing our safety! When we open our hearts to others, their hearts cannot help but notice and appreciate this olive branch. Plus, it's fun! I'm learning new things. I'm experiencing new cultures and new viewpoints! It's fascinating!

Since you are such a skilled protector, I do not wish to retire your services, but I am reassigning you to a new task. Your job is to stay on the lookout for people who are actually dangerous. For example, people holding weapons or using threatening words or body language. People with an intent to harm. These people exist, and I don't want to be so naive as to be walking around, giving every last person the benefit of the doubt. No. Some people should not be messed with. Help me spot these people, listen to your warnings, and get the hell out of there! And when I'm feeling uncomfortable simply due to contact with someone who is different from me, remind me that we have a new strategy now: to make friends, not enemies. To open our hearts and minds, not close them!

I'm looking forward to our continued work together, Thoressa. Thank you for standing guard!

Your friend,
Chelsea

I'm reminded of the practicality of radical inclusivity and compassion whenever I'm guided through a loving-kindness meditation at my meditation center. When we get to the part about sending loving-kindness to difficult people—even people we hate—the teacher will say something like, "Just imagine: If this person were not hurting, if they were truly happy and peaceful, they would have no urge or need to hurt others. Don't imagine for a minute that their hatred and violence does not leave an ugly reverberation in their heart and mind." And isn't that true?

How many times have I done or said something I regret, only to find I cannot fall asleep at night, tossing and turning, reliving my errors? If this is how I feel after rudely raising my eyebrow at a friend, what must be the karmic weight on the souls of corrupt politicians after the carnage they have strewn into the lives of countless innocents? If they could feel their feelings, find the joy of connection to all living beings, have meaningful and true friendships, be a part of a conscious spiritual community, take delight in a small sparrow taking a dirt bath, and practice forgiveness for the harms done to them in their childhood, we would not be in our current political predicaments. And so I truly wish *all* our dear politicians happiness, ease, joy, and equanimity. Wishing a pox on them only hurts me, constricts my heart, and ruins my appetite. Why layer hatred on top of hatred? Shall we heal the world with bitterness and anger? After bearing witness to Alon's, Raya's, and Ma'isha's stories in Israel and Palestine, only love makes any sense.

This formula of "only love" transfers also to the judgments and war raging within my own heart and mind. Whenever life has dealt me a rough hand, or whenever I've made a painful mistake or caught myself in old, self-destructive habits, how would layering self-hatred on top of this help? Shall I heal my wounds through the violence of self-berating inner dialogue? Of course not.

And so, when the Inner Demons show up, shall I slap them and tell them, "Go to hell"? When the Inner Critic comes knocking at the door of my mind, shall I shout, "Leave me alone, you old hag!" and slam the door in her face? Even though these critical voices are hurtful, they are a part of me. Shall I hurt them back? Mahatma Gandhi, in sharing his wisdom on nonviolence, once said, "There is no path to peace. Peace *is* the path." When the voices of anger and blame are so deafening from within and without, can we have the courage to tap into the Ground of Presence and believe that Love is the Way? And not only to believe it, but to *act as if it were true*?

There is a story from Buddhism about an anger-eating demon who sneaks into the hall of King Sakka while the ruler is away. The demon is hungry, and anger and hatred are his food of choice. He knows how to stir up a feast of anger from the king's loyal subjects, who are the devas, or celestial beings. The demon arrogantly sits himself down on the king's throne and declares himself the new ruler.

"You can't do that!" the devas cry in indignation. "That is our Master's seat! Get out, you disgusting creature! Your foul stink has no right to be here!" They are getting quite worked up, because with each angry utterance, the demon grows in size and strength. "We ought to rip you limb from limb!" they continue shouting. "Be gone!" Their blood is collectively beginning to boil; and the evil demon laughs, getting larger and more handsome by the second. He's quite pleased with himself, as he is now well fed.

When King Sakka returns, the devas rush to him to warn him of the terrible news. Honorable Sakka, a fully enlightened being, is not fazed one bit. He calmly enters the great hall, bows, and smiles at the demon. "Welcome, friend!" he says. "Would you like a drink? Tea? Alcohol? Sweet water? Whatever your heart desires!" In the moment of confronting the kindness in Sakka's voice and the generosity in his heart, the demon becomes completely starved, and disappears.

Similarly, we recall the story of the Buddha being tempted by the demon Mara (who represents a slew of difficult thoughts, emotions, and sensations).

That story is so dramatic that I assumed Mara would be vanquished forever after he fled that scene under the Bodhi Tree. So I was shocked to discover that, years after his enlightenment, Mara still came to visit the Buddha from time to time (meaning that the Buddha was still experiencing unwholesome thoughts). As one of my dear Enneagram teachers, Michael Naylor, says, "Rumor has it the Inner Critic is immortal."

What! You mean after years of spiritual practice, gaining wisdom through life experience, and learning to love myself, these little assholes aren't going to go away?!

Nope. Not completely, at least. So how should I relate to them if I know that we are going to be lifelong companions? In the only way that makes any sense: Love, Kindness, Compassion, and Blessing.

Yes. Bless, and do not curse.

This is why I have chosen to write a letter of blessing to each of my Inner Demons. After years of resisting, ignoring, and berating them, I have only watched them grow. When I offer them new roles, back massages, and permission to retire in peace, they disappear (at least for a while). I think it's because they've been so abused that they immediately take me up on my offer to run off to the spa—and I am amazed every time.

But I'm under no illusion that they will stay at the spa forever. We've become fast friends. They'll start to miss me, and they'll be back. And when they return, my line will be, "I see you, Mara. Would you like Earl Grey? Or jasmine green?"

YOUR TURN!
Inner Work Exercise

Love Your Enemy: Let a difficult person come to mind. This may be someone you know personally, or a group in society at large with whom you are angry or annoyed. Then ask yourself, "Who is this anger helping right now? Who is this anger hurting right now?" Notice how ruminating on these angry thoughts disrupts your peace of mind (and maybe even causes physical symptoms, like nausea, anxiety, or tense muscles). What would it be like to be free of this burden of judgment and hatred?

Next, imagine your enemy completely healed and happy, with all of their social, psychological, emotional, and spiritual needs met. Picture them self-realized. How would their behavior or attitude change if this were true? What effects would this have on the people and community around them?

If this feels like too much of a stretch, approach the idea of love for your enemy by imagining them as a precious baby, or as a completely vulnerable person on their deathbed. How does this change your energy toward them? What impact does that change have on you? On your mental health or level of stress?

Now, choose a group of people you have put in the Other category. These are people who you assume are not like you. Try this visualization/meditation for that entire group. Once you can picture them happy, calm, and at peace, imagine walking toward them. Is there a gesture of kindness you can offer? Perhaps a hug, a pat on the back, or a kiss on the forehead? Maybe you even play a game with them? Don't try to control the visualization. As long as you are still feeling safe and open, see what actions and feelings spontaneously emerge. Stay with that feeling of belonging and compassion for as long as you can.

When you are finished, jot down a few notes about how this experience was for you. It's easy to forget about the messages from our heart and soul unless we write them down.

NOTE: This exercise is not meant to condone others' bad behavior, or even to forgive them. Instead, it's meant to shift the negative impacts of our attitude on *us*. Without the anger, we are still capable and free to take wise and skillful action to work toward correcting injustice, abuse, or neglect. We notice that the compassionate approach is also motivating and is more enduring than the expensive fuel of anger. It is here that our inner work begins to fuel our outer work in the world, making us more effective activists, parents, employees, helpers, lovers, and friends.

PART 3
Transform It

CHAPTER 12:
What Do Emotions Have to Do with This?

For human beings, the most daunting challenge is to become fully human. For to become fully human is to become fully divine.
—Father Thomas Keating

"Here they come, those little bitches," I caught myself muttering aloud as I watched two tween punk boys entering the public library. These particular kids are always loud, rambunctious, and appallingly disrespectful and obscene. One day, they even verbally harassed me in a sexual manner. It amazes me. It also amazes me how the librarians seem to be completely at a loss over how to respond to them. I'm here to work and relax, as is everyone else, and my sense of communal harmony and justice is disturbed every time they enter and begin slinging profanity. After the harassment episode, I felt unsafe there, so I contacted the library and told them so. They expelled the two boys from the premises through a formal trespass, meaning they were legally barred from the building for a month. But now that time is up, and they are back.

Yes, it's a complicated and frustrating situation. Yes, wise action needs to be taken. But did thinking of them as "little bitches" make it any better? At the very least, did it console me in any way? Of course not. It only stirred my inner pot of self-pity and indignation. That momentary arising of scathing judgment was there to protect me from what was actually happening deep within my body: fear. It is so easy to get sucked back into the old way of being, thinking, and feeling. The inner sludge loves to be stirred. Default Mode awaits when love is not actively being cultivated.

Perhaps I'll always be this way, living continuously with a judging mind. I'm not sure. Certainly, there are (select few) humans throughout history who have attained such inner freedom that they have perpetually walked the path of peace, compassion, equanimity, kindness, mindfulness, gratitude, and joy. They are an inspiration, a reminder that this is somehow possible. (Think Jesus of Nazareth; Siddhartha Gautama, the Buddha; Dipa Ma; Eckhart Tolle; Mother Teresa; and His Holiness the Dalai Lama.)

Heaven help me, I'm not there yet—and neither is anyone else I have met in person. On some days, that stresses me out and throws me into fits of various forms of judgment and anxiety. On other days, that acknowledgment strikes me as a reason to rejoice, relax, and breathe a sigh of relief. Because this reminds me that I'm truly no better or worse than anyone else. We're all in this murky mess of this thing called life, just trying our best to make our way. We are, all of us, a mishmash of mercy and malevolence.

Sure, this can be disheartening. I've been at this spirituality thing in a serious way now for years—decades even—and I'm *still* a mound of anxious thoughts, compulsions, aversion, irritation, and fear. Why? Why me? *Why, Lord, hast thou forsaken me?*

Of course, I have not been forsaken by anyone but myself. In these moments, I try to remember that I am a human being, not a robot. Feelings are a natural part of the package. Emotions are not failings, character defects, or sins. They are not even a part of our Inner Critic. The Inner Critic comes in as a *response* to our emotions. It blames or shames us for being weak, wishy-washy, or afraid. But feelings are the natural flow of expression of this particular mind and heart, in this particular body and life, in this particular moment. *And it will soon be otherwise.*

What emotion have you ever had that lasted forever? (*crickets*)

If emotions are constantly changing, they cannot be "me." There is no "me" who is angry, depressed, or rude. Because there have also been times when I've experienced feelings of joy, freedom, courage, and gratitude. It's ever-changing, so how can we pin down a fixed, unchanging "me" in the middle of the swirl? Let us not be so stressed when uncomfortable emotions arise, thinking we need to fix them or push them away lest they overtake us. They will transform on their own if we welcome them and explore them as messengers passing through. Feelings, both in their form of emotional energy and bodily sensation, often have something they want to teach us, some information they'd like to impart.

For example, I have often had an uncomfortable feeling when meeting certain people, which I have come to recognize as a frantically waving red flag in my gut. But time and time again, my mind has jumped in with logic to convince me that my feelings are silly: *You have no reason to distrust this person. You've just met them. Don't be rude, Chelsea. At least give them a chance.* And then I find out they are manipulating me to support them in their emotional abuse of their spouse. Or trying to get in my pants. Or stealing my whole collection of CDs. Or dumping all their unresolved trauma on to me. Without fail, my emotions have tried to protect me when my mind didn't know how.

Take feelings of hurt or confusion in a relationship as another example. My autopilot response to such discomfort is, *Why are you so sensitive, Chelsea? You're such an overreactor. Get over it!* What I'm not acknowledging is that these feelings are pointing to needs that are not being met, or boundaries that have been inappropriately broken. Someone said that they would do something important for me, then let me down without apology. A friend is only taking in a relationship instead of reciprocally giving. My partner used language that insulted my appearance. These scenarios threaten my need for support, closeness, and acceptance, respectively. There is no blame or shame in having feelings that arise to point out when a relationship needs adjustment.

The Inner Critic's response to emotions blocks our access to Inner Wisdom and Guidance. Here, it is helpful to invoke the teachings of the Enneagram. This personality typing system helps us see that the ego is often threatened by emotions because they go against our particular self-image. Here are the ways each type self-defines. Notice how having a full range of emotions does not fit in well with each particular self-view:

- **Ones:** I see myself as self-controlled, orderly, and seeking perfection.
- **Twos:** I see myself as helpful, available, and nurturing of others.
- **Threes:** I see myself as productive, efficient, and successful.
- **Fours:** . . . (We'll come back to you. You're unique on this topic.)
- **Fives:** I see myself as detached, intellectual, and objective.
- **Sixes:** I see myself as responsible, reliable, and loyal to others.
- **Sevens:** I see myself as happy, exuberant, and free.
- **Eights:** I see myself as strong, powerful, and in control.
- **Nines:** I see myself as peaceful, calm, and amicable.

Again, if you are new to the Enneagram, you'll notice that you may relate to several of these descriptors. This is because we all have a bit of all the types within us. However, there is one type that is your home base, your default, the space to which you consistently (and compulsively) return. As soon as an emotion arises that does not fit within our particular "self-view," inner alarms go off. The Inner Critic is alerted of your trespassing into forbidden territory and incorrectly deems this emotion a "trespass" in the Biblical sense. (*Sinner! Failure! Weakling! Selfish! Depressive downer! Asshole! THIS IS NOT ACCEPTABLE!*)

Let us return to Enneagram Fours for a moment. Fours are incessantly unique in many ways, with the most obvious way being in how they relate to their emotions. Unlike other types, they do not repress their feelings; and they enjoy experiencing the full range of agony and ecstasy, and everything in between. They find beauty in melancholy, a comfortable space of sadness and longing.

Does this mean that Fours have got their emotional game on lockdown? Sorry, Fours, but no. In many ways, Fours have a leg up on the rest of us in this realm because they are not afraid of their feelings, and they give themselves permission to explore them thoroughly. However, they get themselves in trouble because they overidentify with their feelings. They wallow in them. They are tricked into believing their feelings are facts. They curate moods by orchestrating the conditions to feed and prolong certain emotional states. It doesn't even matter what the emotion is (although melancholy is one of a Four's favorites)! As long as Fours are feeling something deeply, they are up-

WHAT DO EMOTIONS HAVE TO DO WITH THIS?

holding their self-image of being profound, intense, and unique. (*If I'm not intensely feeling something, I am dull and ordinary, and my life is without meaning!*) Thus, their egos lay a trap for them too, by cutting off rational thinking, productive action, and stability.

Even if you are not a Four, you have likely dabbled with this strategy of clinging to certain emotions, even negative ones. No matter what your personality type, the problem does not lie with our emotions. It is our *self-view* that trips us up. In restricting our options on what is an acceptable way to be and feel, our particular self-view limits our humanity. As the prison guard of our Inner Critic beats us back into our familiar box, we revert to default mode, autopilot, and mechanical reactions. We move further from the tender freedom of a human heart and toward robotic numbness. Paradoxically, this distancing from our difficult emotions also distances us from authentic positive emotions. Our hearts cannot choose which emotions to cherry-pick in applying numbness. We open either to all or to none. In shutting out our painful emotions, Spirit death looms just around the corner.

This may sound quite dramatic, yet we needn't be frightened. When we can clearly see that a fixed view of self—of "me"—is at the core of our distress, we naturally relax around our emotions. We no longer need to push them away to maintain a certain self-image. Nor do we need to prolong them, thinking that deep feelings will define us and bring meaning to our lives. How could something impermanent ever define you?

The Spanish language (and perhaps many other languages) is very helpful in making this distinction in impermanence. Spanish has two separate verbs for "I am." *Soy* signifies a permanent state, a fact that doesn't change, like "Soy rubia" ("I am blond") or "Soy de Minnesota" ("I am from Minnesota"). *Estoy* connotes a fluid and temporary sense of "I am." And surprise, surprise—this is the verb tense used to describe emotions, like "Estoy enojada" ("I am angry"). This does not subliminally suggest that I am an angry person as a permanent state of my flawed character. I just happen to be experiencing anger in this moment, and the flexibility within the language helps bring that to light. The same goes with "Estoy deprimida" ("I am feeling depressed right now"). Conversely, English uses the same "I am" for everything, solidifying our sense of "me" (e.g., "I am pissed," "I am poor," "I am impatient"). For many feelings, Spanish can remove the "I am" altogether and use "I have," further distancing this emotion from self-identity. For example, "I am sad" can become "Tengo una tristeza" ("I have sadness"). There is an instant energetic shift with this distinction. It allows me to be connected to this sadness and experience it without being defined by it.

With the scenario of the tween library perps, I quickly transitioned through my snap judgment by admitting that my underlying emotion was fear. There was nothing inappropriate or weak about that anxiety. It was doing its job, alerting me to approaching danger and trying to protect me from harm. Once this was acknowledged, clear thinking emerged. I took proper precautions and locked the door to my study room. I reminded myself that I could talk to the on-site security guard if I witnessed further disruption or disrespectful behavior. I was safe.

Taking a few deep breaths, compassion flooded in and I thought, *Gosh, it's hard being a woman. And gosh darn it, it's also hard being a young boy, trying to figure out how to be a man in this hypermasculine society, trying to impress your friends and fit in, needing to hang out at the library all day because being home isn't a safe option. May those boys find safety and protection. May they learn from their mistakes, and may they find inner peace and stability.*

With my heart open, my body and my mind calmed down. Then I took a few more deep breaths and got back to work.

Why Continue on the Path?

Sometimes I feel that the longer I'm on my spiritual path and the more I commit to self-awareness, the harder life gets. With increased awareness, now I'm actually seeing my ego and my Inner Critic run amok instead of living in numbness and denial. Why embark upon a spiritual path if the result is going to be opening myself to more emotions, continued discomfort, and possibly having the same annoying idiosyncrasies crop up for the rest of my life? Is that old adage true, that "ignorance is bliss"?

WHAT DO EMOTIONS HAVE TO DO WITH THIS?

Of course not. (Oh, dear little ego, stop that. You're trying to trick me into regression.)

Strangely, there is no regressive option. Once you have truly seen and tasted reality, there is no going back. Not completely anyway. If you have picked up this book and read it this far, you have already swallowed the "red pill." Congratulations! You are a true Seeker of Truth. But unlike *The Matrix*'s hero, Neo, you aren't about to wake up into a horror-filled world in desperate need of your salvation. You are slowly waking up to the Light of Awareness and Love within you.

Sometimes insight may come as a flashy *bang!* More often, it will come and continue to come steadily, like watching an endless sunrise. The hues and shapes will continuously change; and at times, ferocious storm clouds will appear. But one thing remains the same as we keep watch: The Light is increasing, coming closer. Its warmth is first felt as a slight caress on the skin. But soon it is penetrating deep into your bones, warming all the frozen and frightened places within, making soft what was held tight, loosening the rigid recesses of your soul. The mind learns to let go. The heart learns to open. The body learns to give, receive, and speak.

Despite the beauty of the spiritual path, storm clouds will still arise to cloud the mind. Hurricane winds will tear at the heart. Floodwaters will rise and threaten to pull us under. But those of us walking the Way of Love have a firm foundation. We shall not be swept away by every worldly wind. There remains the possibility of true Refuge, of standing on that Solid Rock. Because we have been there, we know the way back, and Wisdom Herself will pull us into safe harbor.

There is no promise of an easy life once one undertakes spiritual practice. Old habits and patterns will still show up. However, on my journey, I have noticed the result of my practice is that I no longer wallow in the sludge of my ego self, my unhelpful stories, or painful emotions for as long as I once did. A decade ago, I would stew in a particular resentment or fear for *years*. I would replay the same old tapes in my head, riding the merry-go-round from hell, unable to get off. Internally, I would obsess about how to fix other people, rework old conversations so that they would turn out the way I'd wished, and criticize myself for the same old thing—and then turn around and do that very thing again. I felt doomed to live forever this way.

These days, all these traps still present themselves to me. Sometimes I step into them. The difference is, I *see* myself doing it now. I know where this path leads if I continue following it, and I *get out*. Now I have choices. I have tools. I have developed the patience and presence to love myself enough that I no longer accept the momentum of this "fate." Turns out that it's not fate after all.

I used to believe that I was a judgmental person—and that there was no changing this. Exasperated, I told Greta, my Twelve Step sponsor, about it. Sitting next to a tiny fountain on the patio of our regular coffee shop, I cried frustrated tears. "I'm so sick of it," I said. "I hate the thoughts I have about myself and others. And when I sit down to meditate, it only gets worse, because it's like watching these ugly thoughts under a microscope!"

"And what do you do when those thoughts come up?" Greta asked.

"Push them away. Try to go back to my breath. But a minute later, they're back!"

Greta sat for a moment in silence, slowly turning her coffee mug in a circle. I waited. The trickle of the fountain sounded like a wailing torrent of sorrow.

"Here's your assignment," Greta finally said. "Every time you notice a judging thought, pat yourself on the back. Noticing it is a *good* thing. It means you're paying attention." Then she went on to explain that instead of pushing away difficult thoughts and feelings, we can instead *accept* them. Oftentimes, the acceptance itself dissolves the energy of the thought, and there is no further action to be taken.

This changed everything for me. I didn't have to *do* anything. I didn't have to make it go away or fix myself. I just had to notice it and accept it. Notice, then accept. Acceptance of all parts of ourselves also lets go of the idea that the negative thought or emotion is to be gotten rid of to protect the "me" self-image as someone who should not be feeling this way.

I began to learn how to relax when difficult emotions arose. In this state of relaxation, it became possible to choose a more helpful thought. Perhaps gratitude was an appropriate substitute for criticism. Or maybe it was fierce compassion, or the stabilizing force of equanimity. Either way, these chosen,

WHAT DO EMOTIONS HAVE TO DO WITH THIS?

positive mind states only had a chance of sticking around *after* I accepted my shadowy parts. Trying to push away my shadow by forcing gratitude to appear just feels like a battle. It is disingenuous.

The important thing to remember here is that this is a *process*. Some Inner Critic voices may vanish. Others may weaken over time, and still others are ones you may struggle with for a lifetime. The same goes for difficult emotional patterns. Over time, by applying kind attention and acceptance, some patterns will loosen. They will grow less intense or last for shorter periods. Others will keep showing up again and again. This doesn't mean you're doing life wrong, or that you're incompetent or unspiritual. It just means you're having an emotion. That's it. The more we allow ourselves to feel, the more human we become, and the more our hearts open to ourselves and others.

So stop fighting your emotions. You can't "fix" them, nor should you if you could. They are there for a reason. Feelings are meant to be *felt,* not fixed. Put down the load, let go of resistance, and let it flow!

YOUR TURN!
Inner Work Exercises

1. Change Your Language around Emotions

Practice removing the "I am" from emotional statements. Instead of saying "I am angry" or "I am depressed," try some of the following, and notice how the energy in you shifts when you speak like this:

- "Anger is showing up right now."
- "The mind is really irritated at this moment."
- "This heart is experiencing a lot of sadness today."
- "Anxiety has been visiting me a lot lately."

2. Pat Yourself on the Back When You Notice Undesirable or Unskillful Habits

Truly congratulate yourself, and be happy that your self-awareness is increasing! Use positive self-talk, like these examples below:

- "Wow! Nice job! You just noticed you slipped back into self-deprecation again."
- "There's that criticism again. So great that you saw it and didn't get swept away by it! Yay!"
- "Yep, there's another hateful thought. You get a gold star for self-awareness!"

Go ahead and be silly with it, because if you can get yourself to laugh at the Inner Critic, its power is instantly removed.

3. Practice the Welcoming Prayer

This was originally developed by the Trappist monk Father Thomas Keating. Sit comfortably in a quiet place. Then take three deep breaths, and feel into the sensations of your body. Continue to be open and receptive, not trying to make anything happen.

As you notice thoughts, emotions, and sensations arise, welcome them as you would a beloved guest. Invite them to take off their coat and stay a while. Ask them what they have come to teach you. Sit with your guest(s) and listen. Do not push them away in fear or impatience. Really feel where this emotion or thought pattern shows up in your body. Get to know it.

Finally, ask Godde or your Inner Wisdom or Higher Self if there is any further message to be learned here. Listen again, not forcing answers but rather allowing your holy imagination to run free.

Also, begin and end your time of receptive prayer and meditation by reciting these words by Father Keating:

The Welcoming Prayer
Welcome, welcome, welcome.
I welcome everything that comes to me today because
I know it is for my healing.
I welcome all thoughts, feelings, emotions, persons,
situations, and conditions.
I let go of my desire for power and control.
I let go of my desire for affection, esteem, approval,
and pleasure.
I let go of my desire to change any situation,
condition, person, or myself.
I open to the love and presence of Godde and
Godde's action within.
Amen.

CHAPTER 13:
Spiritual Friendship

We are here to awaken from the illusion of our separateness.
—Thich Nhat Hanh

One time, I woke up on a Sunday morning, and all my bones felt as heavy as cement. I hit Snooze on my alarm and thought, *Please let me sleep this off. Or let me never wake up.* Later, the alarm buzzed again, and I unconsciously turned it off instead of snoozing it. Or was it intentional? What was this dank sadness pinning me to the bed?

The sickness in my belly was easily recognizable. My Inner Critic was up to something menacing. I was hating myself, but I was not feeling my normal, motivating anger. Instead, I was thinking, *What's the point? You've totally ruined your career. You're a horrible facilitator and an even worse person. You robbed all those people of a perfectly good Saturday afternoon! That's time that they can never get back, and a reputation that you can never earn back. Stupid. Just sleep—forever.*

Drifting in and out of consciousness, I tried to direct my mind to sexual fantasies. Anything to not feel this pain. I'd been musing about lucid dreaming lately. Perhaps I could change my mind's course. It didn't work. As exhausting as the feeling was, it wouldn't let me sleep. It was like having a giant anvil on my whole body, my life force being slowly squeezed from my being. It's hard to sleep when you can't breathe. Nowhere to go. No reason to get up. The pressure of the checklist was looming, but it now felt irrelevant after I'd ruined my career.

The day before, I had led an Enneagram workshop for organizers and activists that had been hosted by an organization I admired and respected. Everyone was at different levels in their Enneagram learning; and I had been tasked with emphasizing spiritual practices in relation to Enneagram work, providing activists with a counterweight to all the *doing* and *striving* and *stressing* that is inherent in organizing culture. I had provided that—quite beautifully. I also believe I had given lovely descriptions of all the types that were helpful to even the seasoned Enneagram enthusiasts in the room.

So what was the problem that was weighing me down the following morning, making me feel ready to completely give up my vocation and write myself off as a degenerate? I had mismanaged the time. The last activity I had planned for the workshop participants was left out because we ran out of time. And it was this activity that was the only part that related specifically to activist and organizing work. The capital sin for an Enneagram One had been committed: I had not delivered on my promise.

Even so, I had gotten a lot of great feedback about the workshop. And yet I had still gone home knowing I had made a huge mistake that my Inner Critic would not let me live down. Harsh Grader was breathing down my neck once again. (*Ahh, brr.*) Luckily, I'd had enough momentum of Presence to notice it during and after the workshop, and it hadn't thrown me further off my game. As soon as I had gotten home, I had gone to my yoga mat, laid down in a restorative posture, and begun giving myself a compassionate pep talk.

"You are having a severe Inner Critic attack right now, Chelsea. That's really hard. I'm so sorry it's so hard for you right now," I said out loud, rubbing small, comforting circles on my chest. It was easing the pain a bit. I continued by saying all the rational things I wanted to believe: "You were trying something new, and so of course it didn't go perfectly. This is a wonderful learning opportunity for you. You see clearly where you went wrong, and you will course correct yourself next time. You are a human being, and mistakes are part of that equation. All facilitators go through this at some point. You can't knock all of them out of the park. You did nothing wrong, and it was still a really valuable offering that you provided for these people."

Yes. This was all true. Something inside of me had known all of that, logically. But as the day had gone on, the heaviness had begun to set in; and by Sunday morning, it felt like full-blown depression. (*Everyone knows I'm a phony. A failure. An idiot. I've been advertising myself as an excellent group facilitator, and it's all a lie. You are so deceptive that you even deceived yourself. LIAR!*)

After a day of hearing these internal accusations and responding to them with compassion, I was wondering why the magic of kindness wasn't helping this time. It was time to turn to outside help. I have a small handful of friends who know how to get me out of this state. I have their names saved on a note on my phone. If I didn't have that list, I would forget about these angels in times of distress; and my Inner Critic would have me believe that I am totally alone, doomed to try fixing my mind with my mind.

"Hey," I said to my friend Lynn, my voice cracking. "I need a pep talk. I'm in a dark place."

Lynn is often the exact person I need to save me from myself. With some intuitive gift of heart-wisdom, she can see exactly what is needed and cut straight through to the solution. Somehow, she does all of this without offering advice and trying to fix me, which I love. She just loves me so hard, until I can again see the possibility of loving myself.

Lynn began by offering several ideas about different compassion meditations and visualizations, with both my Inner Child and my Elder Self. But no, that wasn't it. She went on to suggest many ways in which I could make amends to the people at the workshop and somehow provide them with the information they had missed out on that I so desperately wanted them to have. Yes! That was it. This time, the solution was a practical one. I felt as if I had cheated these people and withheld from them the piece they had specifically requested. So the way to alleviate my suffering was to *do* something about it, because there *was* something I could do.

I felt good that I had at least given these folks a handout with some good info on it, but I needed to take it a step further. I emailed them all a thank-you and an apology, with attachments to resources including a blog post I had written just for them. The blog post included my reflections on the Enneagram and how it can specifically benefit activists, as well as a set of reflection questions and exercises they could use to do their own reflection or group conversation. As soon as I sent the email, the burden lifted. Now I could truly say, "I've done all I could do, and I'm letting the rest go."

The interesting part here is that my Inner Critic was, in part, telling me the truth. I had let some of these people down and left a promise unfulfilled. That needed to be addressed to uphold my integrity and professionalism. The problem with this whole thing was that the Inner Critic added so many insults and lies into the mix that I couldn't sort out the tiny bit of truth that needed to be addressed with practical action. It all felt so overwhelming that I assumed the whole mess of it was hogswallop when it wasn't. I was feeling the appropriate emotion of guilt—but my Inner Critic jumped on that, added its extra story, and turned my guilt into shame. It took talking to a trusted friend to parse this out.

Why is it so hard for us humans to admit our insecurities and stuck places to others? Why is it so hard to verbalize our inner obsessions to another? It's complicated. And the answer is likely different for each of us. But it probably has to do with some version of a belief that our vulnerability will be judged or trivialized by others. Or that it will be a burden, an imposition on their serene little bubble. (*Appropriate people don't bother friends with their mess. If you cry in front of them, they'll be uncomfortable. Don't ruin their day. Hold it in.*)

Many of us tend to have so much discomfort with sharing our insecurities with others that when we're asked how we're doing, we often answer, "I'm fine. How are you?" In Twelve Step circles, the acronym FINE stands for "fucked up, insecure, neurotic, and emotional."

Or, perhaps showing the neurotic version of ourselves to others feels like taking off the armor. Exposing our greatest weaknesses will allow others to hit us where it hurts, poke fun, spread gossip, or ruin what shred of good reputation we were holding on to. (*How could I possibly share this fear with someone? They'll find out I'm not enough. I'll come on too strong and be too much. They'll retreat. Or they'll pity me and take me on as their pet project. Fuck that. I don't need saving. I just need to cry.*)

And yet, if we can get over these fears and just spit it out (with a safe person), there is something endlessly healing about hearing our thoughts and feelings as they're witnessed by another person. This is the healing power of the practice of spiritual direction. So often, I'll be sitting with a spiritual direction client, and they will be rambling on and on. I'll barely say anything in a session, yet they will usually end with a huge sigh of relief and a "Thank you." And they keep coming back!

The power of a loving witness amazes me. Yet it does not baffle me, because it makes perfect sense. We are social creatures. While our modern culture isolates us further and further, our evolutionary disposition toward connection, mutual support, and tribal living has not left us. We were made for each other. Friendship is the balm that heals the soul. It is our relatedness that brings us back to reality. With all of our quirks, traumas, and unique personal experiences, we are still remarkably alike at our core. We all experience anger, disappointment, shame, and fear. So when I call up Lynn and say, "My Inner Critic is telling me I just flushed my whole career down the shitter," she can gently smile and say, "I know exactly how you feel," because she's been there too. Even though she has a different temperament, a different family culture, a different Enneagram type, and a different set of life experiences. When I gather up the courage to verbalize my Inner Demons, others give me the grace to realize that I'm not alone, that I'm not as uniquely flawed as I had once thought.

I am perfectly imperfect, and I am imperfectly perfect—and there is something Holy about this. If I never made mistakes or had difficulties, I wouldn't need anyone else: not my friends, my spiritual director, my teachers, or my Higher Power, that Universal Source of love that is ever-present and available to draw from whenever I'm feeling weak. Without my flaws, there would be no need for a relationship. I could coast along alone, solving all my problems, including the problem of being so strongly identified with being a "me" who has "problems." But, fortunately, I can't. I am not a Buddha who will attain enlightenment by finding my way with no teachers. I have leaned on wisdom and guidance from countless hundreds of teachers, authors, mentors, pastors, friends, family members, YouTube personalities, theologians, gurus, passages from various scriptures and spiritual texts, and lessons gleaned from observing Nature Herself. It is delusional to think I am an independent "me." As they say so eloquently in South Africa, "Ubuntu," which means "I am because we are."

Even the Buddha himself had shockingly radical revelations about the importance of community. There he was, bushwhacking his way through the reality of human suffering; tirelessly pursing Dhamma, the way things are; and peeling off layer after layer of greed, anger, and delusion with no teachers to guide him. He was, as he said, "a lamp unto himself." And yet that is not the whole story.

The Buddha had a cousin named Ananda who was one of his attendants, students, and friends. One day, Ananda was contemplating friendship; and he became quite pleased with himself, thinking that he had happened upon a major insight. So he went to the Buddha and said, "Dude. I've been sitting in deep contemplation, thinking about spiritual community and stuff. And man, I get it now, cousin! Check it. I've come to realize what you are throwing down: that spiritual friendship is half of the entire path, man!" Then he waited for his guru to pat him on the head and praise him for his genius.

But the Buddha shook his head, disappointed. He was like, "Yo, Ananda. Bro. You don't get this *at all*. Spiritual friendship is not half the path. It is the *whole path*, man!"

(What you just read is my translation of the story, obviously. Why they sound like surfers here, I'm not sure.)

There are also hundreds of anecdotes I could give from early Christianity about the importance of communal support, of naming our needs to our friends, of asking for help emotionally, physically, and spiritually. The early church depicted in the Book of Acts was basically a socialist intentional community. Everyone pooled their resources and parsed them out evenly among themselves. There was great emphasis from Jesus himself on asking for what you need: "Ask and it will be given to you; seek and you will find; knock and the door will be opened to you. For everyone who asks receives; the one who seeks finds; and to the one who knocks, the door will be opened" (Matthew 7:7–8).

The cycle of giving and receiving was not just given lip service in early Christian communities. The act of generosity was actively practiced. I do not think that Jesus was speaking of supplicative prayer in this verse. I believe he was being quite literal. Why do we always twist his words around to mean something different from what is said? Why has the "it" being asked for come to mean "salvation in the afterlife" instead of a hug, a listening ear, or twenty bucks? Why has "the door" been interpreted as the door into heaven instead of the door of a neighbor or a friend opening to someone in distress?

Even Jesus himself had needs and asked for them. He often asked his disciples to leave him alone so he could have some time to himself to recuperate from his intense ministry of being a traveling healer and a rabbi. Sometimes he asked a few of his best friends to come with him on hikes up to mountaintops, or to quiet gardens where they could pray in peace. One time, right before his arrest, trial, and execution, he asked his friends to stay awake with him and pray for him. They kept falling asleep, and Jesus got upset about it. I can just imagine him thinking, *I've been giving, giving, GIVING to you bums nonstop over the last three years! Free wine! Free loaves and fishes! Saving your stupid asses from drowning in storms on the boat, and you can't even send me some good juju right before I die?* Despair must have set in then. This whole time, Jesus had thought his friends were getting it, understanding that spiritual friendship is *the whole of the path*. But there they were, snoring away in his hour of greatest need.

Luckily, they redeemed themselves after he died. They split up and set about the task of establishing intentional spiritual communities all over the Middle East. They taught these communities how to mediate conflict, how to share resources, how to pray for one another, how to listen to one another, how to forgive one another. They called this "casting out demons."

Social isolation, exaggerated individualism, materialism, an "us verses them" mentality, and a lauded sense of self-sufficiency are now our modern-day communal demons. To cast them out and transform our collective "sins," we must begin by risking vulnerability. We must be willing to name our needs, our mistakes, our destructive thought patterns, and the influence of our Inner Critics. In a way, our Inner Critics are part of a sickened collective consciousness. The good news is that this consciousness can be swayed. We need not suffer alone and in silence. When we verbalize our suffering to a trusted friend, the pain eases. The knots in our minds loosen. The shame dissipates. Why wait for someone else to change the culture? We, along with our friends, can begin tipping the scales of staunch independence toward a beautiful flow of interdependence.

It has been quoted so heavily now that it has almost lost its meaning, but I risk quoting Gandhi again when he implores us, "Be the change you wish to see in this world." That can feel daunting. How could I ever live up to Gandhi's legacy? But that's not what he's asking. Every small shift in our personal choices *matters*.

It matters when we choose to call a friend to say, "I really need to thrash around and cry right now, and I need you to just listen."

It matters when we follow our intuition to offer help to a friend or stranger. It is not imposing on them to offer. They can always say no if it's not what they need or want.

It matters when we choose to respond with kindness to ourselves instead of with hatred.

It matters that we ask, seek, and knock.

It matters that we each learn to humbly receive.

It matters that we become a soul friend to someone and that we gather spiritual friends around us.

You matter.

I matter.

They matter.

We matter.

Every time I head out the door after a spiritual direction session, my loving friend and spiritual director Janet says, "Keep drinking from deeper wells." She has been saying this to me for ten years, and I am only now beginning to really understand what this means. Truth be told, I never thought about it too much until a short while ago.

The term "deeper wells" suggests that there are shallow wells to drink from. I certainly am familiar with those. After drinking from them, I am left thirstier than ever before. Here are some places I've run to in search of a lasting quench to my dissatisfaction with life:
- Striving to be above reproach
- Being admired and approved of by others
- Earning the respect of people I care about
- Helping others with their problems
- Making myself needed
- Getting a GPA above 4.0
- Fantasizing about and searching for a career that will fulfill me completely
- Curating certain "moods" to wallow in
- Eating ice cream
- Eating dark chocolate
- Becoming knowledgeable on certain topics
- Looking at things from an objective and logical perspective
- Repressing my emotions
- Filling up my life with stimulating and pleasurable activities
- Getting a dog
- Living in a community
- Drinking coffee
- Searching for a life partner
- Trying to fix my current partner
- Treating myself like a self-improvement project
- Having a plan and being prepared
- Making checklists
- Worrying
- Venting and raging
- Buying a kick-ass bike
- Upgrading to an electric bike
- Saving money for my future
- Numbing out through books and movies

- Checking Facebook
- Eating more chocolate
- Checking Facebook again
- Thinking about making popcorn
- Slicing a pear and spritzing it with just the right amount of salt, lemon, and chili powder
- Obsessing over plucking my eyebrows
- Watching *The Daily Show* and Trevor Noah's stand-up
- Buying new shoes
- Explaining why I'm right and you're wrong
- Cleaning my house
- Being in a position of power
- Trying to save all the children at the school I work at from their horrible manners and trauma
- Having a bomb-ass hairdo

As legend has it, the Buddha held up two leaves while teaching his students one day and said, "There are innumerable leaves in this forest, and yet I hold only two. Just so, while there are innumerable things I could teach, I choose to teach only two: suffering, and the end of suffering." (Again, my paraphrasing.) The Buddha didn't choose this focus to be a stick-in-the-mud. He chose it because the study of the roots of suffering leads to seeing suffering clearly, as it truly is—and that leads to liberation.

But instead of getting curious about the persistent dissatisfaction inherent in living a life, we keep trying things that we have temporarily convinced ourselves will ultimately satisfy. Some days, I just *know,* with all my might, that eating that gourmet, eight-dollar ice cream cone is going to make me happy. So I go out and buy it; and before I'm even half way through eating it, I feel sick both physically and emotionally. The "happiness" lasted for about the first three licks. It turns out that *nothing* in this life satisfies. Not permanently anyway. Because everything is always changing. If I ever find the "perfect" life partner for me, I know they will not fulfill me. There will be days when they are the source of my deepest suffering. It's a setup for believing the story about "happily ever after." And yet, I do. (*If I could just travel to all my bucket-list va-*

cation destinations, then I'd be happy. If I could just have perfect health, then I'd be happy. If I could just find a way to make more money, then I'd be happy. . . .)

One needn't be a Buddhist to get interested in suffering. All we need is curiosity about our patterned lives and personalities, the willingness to be brutally honest about what we discover, and the openness to let go of our viewpoints. That, of course, is much easier said than done, since our defense mechanisms and incredible capability to live in denial are so strong. This is why it is helpful to have a wise guide, a teacher, a holistic therapist, or a spiritual director. Best to have one of each, because most of us need all the help we can get! At least I do.

These healers, mentors, and spiritual guides can help us course correct when we insist on drinking from shallow wells. They remind us that there is another source—*the* Source—that comes from a much deeper place, satisfies the soul, and aids us in our journey through suffering.

All this talk of wells has got me thinking of the story of Jesus speaking with the Samaritan woman at the well. Provocatively, he tells her he can offer her Living Water. Wondering what he means by this bizarre statement, she prods him further; and he answers her, "Everyone who drinks this water will be thirsty again, but whoever drinks the water I give them will never thirst. Indeed, the water I give them will become in them a spring of water welling up to eternal life" (John 4:13–14). What in Godde's name did he mean by that?

I do not propose to have *the* answer. I know what the answer is for me, at least partially. There are many ways in which I've found access to the Deeper Well. While I have not yet found how to remain connected to the Living Water at all times (because my active ego still lures me away from it), when I do drink of it, I sense that it has been waiting for me to receive it—waiting for me beyond space and time, in this mysterious space called Eternity. Its flavor is patience and grace, joy and abundance, kindness and immeasurable Love. And just like the Samaritan woman at the well, it often comes to me in the form of a friend with whom I share a drink.

I'll close this chapter with the lyrics of a song that I sang in a gospel choir while in college. I could hardly ever get through this song without breaking down into happy tears. What a blessed release, to admit my needs and vulnerabilities! I need help, Hallelujah!

> I need you, you need me
>
> We're all a part of Godde's body
>
> Stand with me, agree with me
>
> We're all a part of Godde's body
>
> It is Godde's will that every need be supplied
>
> You are important to me, I need you to survive.[9]

YOUR TURN!
Inner Work Exercises

1. Make Phone Calls

In Twelve Step communities, one of the suggested tools of the program is making phone calls to another community member when one is feeling distressed or caught in obsessive thinking. Just verbalizing our pain out loud and hearing loving feedback from another person who understands us often reduces—if not completely alleviates—the struggle.

Take a few moments to make a list of trusted friends or mentors you can call when you are struggling. Put this list somewhere where you will see it frequently, and/or save it on your phone lest you forget that these supports exist when in the throes of an obsessive track of thinking. You can even ask friends if you can put them on this list. It's likely that they will be thrilled to be on the list and even happier if you actually call. People love offering help to others. Give them the gift of the chance to support you! And tell them they can call you too. What a glorious possibility!

When you call, you don't need to plan out what you are going to say ahead of time, as awkward as this call may feel. Just take a few deep breaths, set the intention to be honest, and dial the number. If they don't answer, leave a voice mail and/or call someone else. Even leaving a voice mail staves off the Inner Critic, because it knows it's going to be exposed, so it starts to behave. Then you are accountable for following through with your intention.

2. Find a Spiritual Director and/or Therapist

A spiritual director is a soul friend who accompanies a person through the path of spiritual discovery, joy and pain, questions and doubts. It's a loving, nonjudgmental process that allows a person to acknowledge their wounds and enter a space of healing. The core work of spiritual direction supports people in deepening their trust in a loving God, Goodness, or Goddess, and in listening and noticing where Spirit is leading and showing up. Spiritual direction is different from therapy or coaching in that the aim is not to "fix" you or accomplish goals. The process is about pursuing continued spiritual freedom and a deepening sense of loving relationship with self, community, and Godde.

The spiritual director helps in pointing out what is real (e.g., the elements of your Essence) verses what is false (e.g., your stories, fears, or personality). All parts of life are suitable topics in spiritual direction, since the things that affect our hearts, minds, and bodies inevitably affect the Essence of our being (our spirits or souls). Spiritual directors work with people of all faiths or none. This relationship with a trained listener is unique and can offer a much-needed space in our lives, a space that friends and family usually cannot fill because they have a personal investment in influencing us in certain directions.

To find a spiritual director who is right for you, visit www.sdiworld.org and click on "Find a Spiritual Companion." Many spiritual directors will provide the option to meet with people remotely via online video platforms, so this opens up the possibility to find the right spiritual director for you regardless of their location.

CHAPTER 14:
Emergence of the Inner Advocate

Perhaps all the dragons in our lives are princesses who are only waiting to see us act, just once, with beauty and courage. Perhaps everything that frightens us is, in its deepest essence, something helpless that wants our love.
—Rainer Maria Rilke

As I hear the rain pitter-patter on the tent fly, a coolness in temperature suddenly sweeps in. It is welcome. I begin to actually listen to the rain: soft, tender, embracing the sacred land with care and nourishment. My head itches and I reach to scratch it, wondering if I have any wood ticks attached to me. Even if I do, this moment feels steeped in blessing, an immediate receiving of Presence. Being fully immersed in the moment—and just being—I know this is a memory that I will not forget until my long-term memory fails me.

There is a blessed release in just listening. In being receptive. In just breathing. In opening my heart to the rhythm of the One, the dance of Mother Nature attending to all her children: me; Chancho; my friend Mel, cuddled in her sleeping bag; the obnoxious pot-smoking neighbors in their huge RV; the forest; the trickling Middle River; the water bugs; the slew of tadpoles along the edge of the swimming hole.

When I let go and lose myself in Her embrace, it opens the way to Love. Kind Inner Voices, long locked away and violently shoved into my innermost recesses, find their way to the surface. Presence prepares the Way, making flat the mountains of my ego and raising the valleys of sublime emptiness. I am sensitive to all the sensations of my body as my heart comes out of hiding. This heart, now free to feel whatever is true, is like cupping a baby bunny in my hands. Soft and tender, vulnerable. Its beauty stirs in me an awe that would have taken my breath away if my breath had not already settled into a slow tempo of supportive holding. With my heart open and free, my mind lets go of the need to run stories about who I am. The silence between thoughts lengthens, and I listen to it. It is the balm of Consciousness itself.

From this place of interior stillness rises the voice of the Inner Advocate: *Peace, be still.* Without words, she conveys her message: *May you be happy and healthy, safe and protected. May you be a friend to your body. May goodness and mercy follow you all the days of your life, and may you dwell in the house of Wisdom forever.* She says . . . nothing. She listens. To my breathing. To the innermost heart of my heart. She is my soul. With a mysterious language of Presence, she conveys this message: *You are loved. You are love.* The breath breathes the magical taste of heaven, in and out. In. Out.

The first few times this happened to me, it was amazing to witness something compassionate welling up from within. To discover I housed inherent blessings, wisdom, guidance, encouragement, and love was quite the shocker. I'm sure by now you can understand why. With such a cacophony of Inner Critics, the first time a clear and positive voice rang forth from within, I was in awe—and giddy with relief. I was not a horrible person after all! There was some pure Essence underneath my thoughts, behind my personality, that had been waiting for me all along. The feeling of gratitude quickly turned to hilarity when this Inner Advocate character revealed his identity.

Here's how it happened. We'll need to rewind to a few months before that moment of peace in the tent.

During a session, I was watching my therapist's fingers move back and forth in front of my eyes while bringing to mind a particular traumatic memory and watching for any thoughts or sensations that popped up. I had been receiving Eye Movement Desensitization and Reprocessing (EMDR) therapy for about six months from a gorgeous young woman named Michelle, trusting this mysterious method would eventually bear fruit. I didn't know what to expect, but I knew that other types of therapy were not moving this certain piece of my mind that was stuck. I didn't even believe it anymore, but the trauma of having internalized an image of a judging and punishing God at a young age was locked in my body, in real and physical ways. Conceptually, I was certain this dread of Godly condemnation was the reason for my chronically sore shoulders and neck, for my desperate attempts at controlling my impulses, and (most dramatically) for my vaginismus. My mind and heart had connected with a Loving Divine Presence, but my vagina was still not convinced. It was still trying to protect me from damnation by locking its doors. This is how I knew it was trauma—and why I had sought out EMDR.

EMDR is a therapy that heals people's brains and bodies from the effects of trauma, be it acute one-time trauma or ongoing microtraumas accrued throughout our developing years. Michelle explained to me that talk therapy had not cured me because the problem wasn't with my mind (i.e., the way I was thinking) but with my *brain.* Certain beliefs and memories were being stored in the wrong place in my brain, which made it feel like I was physically reliving them every time I got triggered. These memories needed to be *physically* moved to the other side of my brain, where I could experience them as true *memories*, as something from the *past* from which I could detach.

Thank Godde! I thought. *There's nothing wrong with me after all!* Just having this little piece of information about the difference between the mind and the brain removed a layer of shame I didn't even know I was carrying. So I came back week after week to conjure up painful, fearful, and shameful memories while Michelle waved her fingers back and forth sixteen inches in front of my face, my eyeballs following their movement. Sure, it was weird, but I had to try it.

The thing that pushed me over the edge and forced me to seek out EMDR was when I'd had a panic attack in church. I had finally found a Christian community I wanted to be a part of. Their focus was on environmental justice, inner work and healing, and raising the voices and experiences of people of color and LGBTQ folks. There was only one problem: The music they sang sounded just like the music I had been so steeped in during my teenage years of damaging religious fundamentalism. Intellectually, I knew these were not the same people with the same theology from my childhood, but my body would not listen to reason. My heart took off around the track of flight, while the rest of my body decided to stay and fight. These opposing energies stole the breath right out of my lungs. I was trying to play it cool, even while hot tears began streaming down my face. *Hold it together, Chelsea*, I'd thought. *You're not in any real danger.* I was sure everyone could hear the drumming of my heart overriding the beat of the music.

While this triggered physiological response may seem irrational at first glance, it was actually my body's innate intelligence screaming for my attention: *Deal with this! Stop repressing your emotions! You deserve freedom!* There was no choice but to listen. I was fed up with this old religious trauma sneaking up on me when I least expected it. I'd had panic attacks at other churches in the past, but I'd written it off because the theological language in those churches gave me the heebie-jeebies, so it made sense that I would react. But here, in this new and safe community I had chosen, it made no sense.

After I'd gone through several months of Michelle's finger-waving, Michelle suggested I listen to some old "praise and worship" music from my teenage years and notice how my mind and body responded. I went home, opened YouTube, and turned on the "Top 20 Christian Hits from 2001" playlist. I waited. Nothing. I even started singing along with a smile on my face. There were moments of nostalgia, but mostly I was bored. I found myself moving around the house, looking for the next thing to do. I wasn't tuning out the music or the lyrics. They just weren't affecting me. Perhaps Michelle's finger-waving was working!

I went back to her office and shared the good news. But there was still more work to do around sexual shame and repression, so we jumped back into the therapeutic routine. Midway through the session, right in the middle of recalling the ways I had been taught to hate my body, a voice rang out from the depths of my mind, piercing through the fog: *That was then. This is now! You have choices!*

Its peppy voice caught me off guard. It had welled up from a deep, spacious place within me, a place I could not locate. Was it my mind? My heart?

My soul? One thing I knew for certain was that this was a new part of me that felt like uncharted territory. Unlike a mantra or positive affirmation, I did not try to conjure or force this cheerful voice. It just *happened*. It was both joy-filled and grounded in confidence.

Later, Michelle asked me, "What are you noticing now?" and I told her about the voice. "Wow! You have an inner pep talker!" she said, laughing. She knew about my practice of naming and picturing the voices in my head, so she asked who this voice was.

"He is a flamboyant little gnome named Sharpakyrie," I answered. How that came to me, I have no idea. But I knew he was very familiar. Even though his voice had never clearly risen above the din of the Inner Critic Committee, this voice instantly felt like Home. It felt like a return to innocence and purity. I sensed I had known Sharpakyrie as a young girl but had forgotten him over the years. And instead of creating a mental reaction that had my mind running in circles, Sharpakyrie's voice was followed by a sweet inner stillness and silence.

While this voice arose with the help of EMDR, I know it was a seed I had been watering and tending for more than a decade. Years of spiritual direction; connecting with my body through dance and yoga; getting curious about observing my mind through meditation; processing my emotions through art, poetry, and songwriting; and practicing surrender through various forms of contemplative prayer had prepared me for this possibility. Now that I know this Inner Advocate is available, I know right where to find it. Its self-revealing was a moment of pure grace, but now that it has broken through the inner racket and into my consciousness, a path has been cleared—a path that I can now choose to follow back into the inner spaciousness of self-compassion.

Years of inner work were finally bearing fruit. It was worth the wait. As Janet, my longtime spiritual director, likes to say, "Joy emerges from pain well attended."

YOUR TURN!
Inner Work Exercises

1. Give Yourself a Pep Talk from Your Inner Advocate

Practicing this when you are already feeling great (or at least in a neutral state) is a good time to allow your Higher Self to speak its truth. Write it out, or speak it aloud. Record the pep talk so that you can return to it when you're feeling down or in the middle of an Inner Critic attack. Tell yourself whatever you most need to hear. You deserve to feel good about yourself not just on a surface level, but also deep down. Start practicing today! With time, this voice will feel louder, more natural, and more authentic than the Inner Critic.

2. Develop a Practice of Using Positive Affirmations

Instead of allowing our minds to dominate and control us with negative messaging, we can choose to replace those thoughts with positive affirmations. These are short statements phrased in a positive way. For example, "I have everything I need and am provided for" is worded positively, whereas "I want to stop worrying" still emphasizes the negative. The affirmations we use should also be *true*. They are things we want to believe that we know are possible. This is not about making a wish list by trying to force the Universe to give us gifts (e.g., "I have a new Lamborghini"). It is about bringing our attention to the gifts already present.

Now, a word of caution to people who already have very optimistic personalities and are continuously reframing negatives into positives, like Enneagram Twos, Sevens, and Nines: Affirmations are *not* about escaping or bypassing our difficult emotions, but they often get misused in this way. Painful emotions are not an indicator that you are failing or defective, and affirmations should not be used as a tool for repression. They are about building our self-love, sense of safety, and confidence while allowing ourselves to feel the full spectrum of human emotion.

Write out a few positive affirmations that counter the stories your Inner Critic tells you. What do you want to believe? Here are a few to get you started:

a. "I am forgiving of myself and others."

b. "I am confident and can stand up for myself."

c. "I trust in Divine timing and provision."

d. "Even though I'm imperfect, I love and accept myself."

Now, place these short phrases around your home where you will see them frequently. (The bathroom mirror, your nightstand, or your work desk are good locations.) Repeat these affirmations in your head or aloud, and perhaps place your hand on your heart and take a deep breath. This quick "reset" is often enough to remind your Inner Critic of who is in charge now (you!). Affirmations give the mind something positive to focus on instead of running its old programming. Over time, and with repetition, we begin to actually believe these positive affirmations!

CHAPTER 15:
The End of an Era

*Be patient. You'll know when it's time for
you to wake up and move ahead.*
—Ram Dass

Turns out miracles do happen.

I woke up the morning of August 28, 2019, and didn't eat my usual breakfast. In fact, I ate no breakfast at all because I knew I would feel slightly nauseous for approximately the next five hours. I had arrived the night before at a gorgeous little cabin in the northern Wisconsin woods, nestled away on the banks of a friendly river bend in a secluded cathedral of pines. All around the house were little statues of Buddhas, rock cairns, and subtle Japanese gardens. The inside of the cabin felt like coming home to myself; I was free to finally let go of all my to-do lists, stresses, and that damn thing called "my story." This was a place where I didn't need to subconsciously worry about what grimacing face I make when I concentrate or cry. A place where I could be alone with my wounds, my animal instincts, and my Higher Power. I was here to ask for complete and total healing from my vaginismus, once and for all.

Sitting on the living room couch, I prepared the space. Drawing one card from a Zen koan deck, one from a deck of verses of the Tao Te Ching, and one from a series of paintings on spiritual themes, I laid them out in front of me on the heavy wooden coffee table next to a box filled with rocks, feathers, and pine cones. The koan card read, "Who is asking?" The Tao card was about governing a nation using as little control as possible, trusting that people do better with fewer rules. The painting card read, "Renew your orbit," and had a series of wild circles spinning out of control. I didn't know yet how any of them would relate to the trip I was about to take, but I'd experienced enough weird synchronicities before then to trust that it was all relevant and that there was an innate Presence within me that knew what I truly needed, even though I had no clue what that was. The Inner Healer had been nudging me, letting me know that it was time for this leap. And I listened. The Inner Healer's voice had become louder than the Inner Critic's. I was tired of beating myself up over things I could not control.

There were two more things to prepare. First, I set out my vaginal dilator set, an attractive tool kit of pastel-colored silicone inserts. The medium size was Creamsicle orange, the large was sky blue, and the jumbo was lavender. They made a cute row of Easter-colored faux penises with my water-based lube at the end. I didn't set out the two smallest sizes, as I had gotten to a point in my practice over the last decade where my vagina could easily receive those with no effort or pain. It was the larger ones—the ones that resembled the size range of real penises—that consistently put my vag on lockdown. But not that day, Satan! That day, with a little (or a lot!) of help from my dear friend psilocybin, I would conquer the lavender penis, so help me Godde!

Psilocybin is the naturally occurring psychedelic compound found in many species of mushrooms. Never in a million years would my younger self have guessed that I'd eventually use psychedelics as a healing modality. I used to think those types of drugs were reserved for freewheeling hippies who had no sense of direction or purpose in their lives, reckless fools who had no sense of self-preservation or morals. Fortunately, one of my more quirky and open-minded friends, Michael, had been slowly introducing me to the healing potential of psychedelics. He told me how they were used in therapy to heal things like depression, anxiety, addiction, and PTSD. But what perked up my ears the most was when Michael started talking about how psychedelics can illicit mystical and spiritual experiences—direct connection with our Essence, with Godde, and with an overwhelming sense of compassion and self-love. I was intrigued. Since these mushrooms grow naturally, and since they have also been used by Indigenous cultures for thousands of years, I was open to it. I tend to be more skeptical of chemical compounds like LSD that are created in labs.

The first time Michael and I had eaten magic mushrooms together, it was a beautiful experience. My perception of my self, nature, and the whole world opened up. I felt connected to everything and fell in love with the rocks, grass, and trees all around me. It felt safe and nurturing, being that we were in a quiet and controlled setting and had prepared our minds to receive the medicine through the setting of intentions and meditation. At the end of this "trip," I felt certain I had only glimpsed a small sliver of what these little mushrooms could do for me. Over the next couple of years, I learned all I could about this substance and its healing properties. Eventually, I was ready to apply their inherent wisdom and guidance to my struggles with vaginismus.

Let us now return to the cabin in the woods surrounded by Japanese gardens. I was almost ready. There was one last thing to prepare: the sacrament itself.

I squeezed some honey into the bottom of the artisan ceramic mug, then added the hot water and a green tea bag. Next, I added the psychedelic mushrooms and stirred. According to measurement charts, I had chosen a large dose. With slow breathing and mindfulness, I walked back to the couch, watching the dried mushrooms slowly expand as their shriveled bodies rehydrated. In the five minutes before drinking the elixir, I reviewed my intentions, getting my head in the right space to have a positive trip:

- "Do not follow the mind's pathways toward paranoia, but remain open to intuition, knowing when there is a true calling to turn toward your fears."
- "If things get too scary, you can choose to change the channel."
- "Trust the medicine. It will take you on unexpected journeys. You think you know how this is going to shake out, but Spirit has something much better in store for you."
- "Stay open. Let go."
- "Release the journey and the results of this trip into Loving Hands."

- "I am open to complete and total healing from vaginismus. I am fully ready to release my story and my identity around this particular form of suffering."

Something deep within me knew this last intention to be true.

I had carried this identity of "sexually dysfunctional woman" with me for long enough. In some ways, it had helped protect me; it had helped me weed out men who didn't have patience or compassion. One miracle of my story is that I'd found men who *did* wait. A couple of them were sweet and caring, and my condition helped them admit they had sexual struggles of their own to work through as well. My partner T was the first person to have the patience and compassion to work through my vaginismus *with* me. He carried my copy of *Completely Overcome Vaginismus* in his backpack for a week and read the whole thing cover to cover. He wanted to understand so that he could help. And he did! At age twenty-nine, I was finally relieved of my virginal status. It was a beautiful moment, filled with gentleness and love. I remember how, the following morning, I flipped back one year in my journal and found the entry that read, "I did it!! I inserted this Q-tip in my vag without pain!!!!" How far I'd come. But sex still wasn't easy.

While vaginismus brought me the blessing of finding a few good partners, I was ready to be done with that particular blessing. (Not the blessing of finding good partners, but of having sexual intimacy that involved dilators, making it still feel a bit like a medical procedure.) A year into my active sexual life, I went to a Mayan Abdominal Massage therapist to help me work out the tension and knots in my pelvic floor muscles. This type of therapy involves massaging the abdominal muscles to restore them to their natural balance and to shift internal organs into their proper position. I was desperate to try anything, thinking perhaps there was something physical to my pain after all. After three sessions, the massage therapist told me she suspected my affliction was much more mental than physical, and she recommended EMDR therapy. She said the traumas of my childhood were still controlling my muscles involuntarily, sending them into a fight-flight-freeze response. I then spent a year in EMDR, attempting to undo all the minitraumas that had accumulated into the associations of "sex equals sin" and "my body equals dirty."

While none of that had magically cured me like I had hoped it would, all that legwork was not a waste of my time. Like John the Baptist preparing the way for Jesus's coming, all of this work prepared the way for the gorgeous mushrooms to work their magic. That decade of working toward sexual freedom had brought me to this moment. Something had shifted in me. I knew I was done with it. There was still a glitch in my brain blocking the control switch on my pelvic floor, but I was confident that this mushroom knew the way through my neural pathways to find the exact spot that needed releasing. (Or erasing. Or rewiring.) I didn't really need to understand *how* it would do this. I just sensed that it *would*. I trusted, in every cell of my body, that this medicine would hold me in the highest form of Grace, intending to heal me in ways I couldn't even imagine.

So I drank it. Slowly. Then I ate the slimy little shrooms. They were less than delicious, but the honey helped.

And then I waited.

I expected the room to start swimming, since that was what had happened to me the last time psilocybin flooded my brain four years before. Back then, all my hallucinations had been visual. It was a stunning beauty to see the shifting fractals in all of nature's patterns, to see the souls of trees and the Earth herself with a heightened vibrancy. I'd become boundless joy, experiencing myself as kin and lover to the Spirit of all nature. I could feel Her feelings and intuit on a deep level how all of life was interconnected, how every little thing I did mattered and made an impact.

But now, sitting on the couch in Wisconsin, nothing was happening. Dozens of flies were buzzing around me, but everything still looked the same. Until I closed my eyes.

BOOM! It was like being thrust into a fast-paced action film. Everything was moving, dark, sinister. I opened my eyes. *Yep, still in the room*, I thought. *Still in my body. I'm safe. Trust the medicine.*

I knew I had to get away from the pesky flies, so I brought a blanket and my water bottle out to the screened-in porch, laid down, and covered myself from the cold. Then I briefly closed my eyes. In the grimy darkness, giant erect penises surrounded me, swirling pools of damning pleasure. I opened my eyes again. Saw the leaves of the trees blowing in the cold wind along the river. *Note to self*, I thought. *If it gets too intense, just open your eyes and take a break. All right. You can do this. For some reason, this is the path that you need to travel right now, into the slimy hell of Penis Land. You can do this.* I shut my eyes and dove back in.

As I continued to be bombarded with sexual images, I allowed myself to feel the fear and repulsion rising within me. Amazingly, I could feel and observe these reactions from a safe space deep within myself, from the seat of the Inner Observer. At some point, it became comical. I saw a sinister creature conducting this disembodied pile of lust, and out of my mouth came the words, "You can't trick me anymore, Satan. I know that sex isn't like this! It's not sinful or gross or scary. It is beautiful, playful, and healing. You have no more role to play in the realm of my sexuality! You are banned from my heart, mind, and body!" And I banished him back to Hell, locked away under the floor, where he looked very disappointed. Sometimes love is fierce; and this time around, I had to tell this particular Inner Demon to go fly a fucking kite.

(I'll pause here to mention that I hesitated to tell you this story. Exorcism? Satan with marionette penises? I realize you may be thinking, *Give me a break, Chelsea. Now you've gone too far!* But it makes perfect sense. We relate to the world through stories, images, and metaphors. We are primarily visual creatures. So, of course, this was exactly what I needed to see: my old stories locked away while I threw the key into the river.)

Back in the cabin's screened-in porch, I got up and danced a little jig. "Satan was here, and I told him to leave, and he left!" I suddenly felt a sense of autonomy over my body and sexuality. Things were beginning to shift.

Many other strange and beautiful things happened over the next four hours, including witnessing the birth of the entire universe and having an orgasm with it. (Don't be too jealous.) Out of this vision, I was given this mantra: "Whatever is within me to receive, I receive it."

I realized suddenly that sex had been all about *giving* for me. Fully receiving was something I had not yet practiced. This was true in almost every part of my life, not just with physical intimacy. Being the Giver maintained the illusion of control. If I was the Giver, I didn't owe anyone anything. I wasn't

THE END OF AN ERA

beholden to anyone. I felt independent, autonomous. It was a brilliant defense against my fear of being manipulated and used. No wonder I had lived like this for so long! And it had worked—until it didn't anymore. Life and relationships were not meant to be experienced as one transaction after another.

Mushroom trips can be funny. I don't just mean funny as in *ironic*, but as in *hilarious*. While they can communicate deep truths and spiritual insights, they often accomplish this through fantastical imagery, playfulness, and humor. It is a gift of pure grace to allow us to see all our ego's tricks from the vantage point of Love itself. The medicine uncovered all my neurotic patterns and lies of separation and allowed me to see them clearly without my normal reactions of shame, anger, or fear. Psilocybin has a gentleness to it, like the sweet healing hands of Jesus or the compassionate smile of the Buddha.

About halfway through my trip, I got off the couch, drank some water to stay hydrated (self-care!), and walked to the bathroom. On my way there, I saw my Easter-colored dilators lined up on the coffee table. I pointed at them, giggled, and proclaimed in a goofy voice, "Irrelevant!" At that moment, I knew without a doubt that my pelvic floor muscles would obey my mind from there on out. The mysterious block in my brain had been broken, and I no longer needed the physical practice. While sitting on the toilet, still giggling with relief and gratitude, I stated my new truth: "When I think I am open, I am open! And there is physical proof: pee comes out!" I was having a grand ol' time by then. My sillies were on a roll.

Looking up at the picture of Krishna and Lakshmi above the sink, I said, "Excuse me, sir. Lord Krishna, you have a penis on your head! And your wife has a sacred vagina in her chest!" In the absurdity of that moment, something clicked within me. I suddenly saw the vagina for what it represented spiritually: the ability to fully receive. I knew then that the act of receiving was just as holy as the act of giving. One could not exist without the other. This is what the word *dana*, from the Pali language of the Buddha's original teachings, is pointing to. When roughly translated, *dana* means "generosity." It is the endless cycle of freely giving and freely receiving that allows relationships and communities to flourish. The key word here is *freely*.

In my Buddhist sangha (or spiritual community), all of the programs, classes, and retreats are offered freely, and people are invited to give any amount that *feels good* for them. If we give too much, that adds stress to our lives. If we give too little, we rob ourselves of the satisfaction and joy of contributing to something beautiful. The amount given is not the focus, because each of us is in a different economic circumstance and we adjust our giving accordingly. The invitation is to notice the tone of the feeling after we give. Does our heart expand or contract after making a certain choice? Do we feel the tightness of stinginess, greed, or a fear of scarcity? Just notice, and adjust accordingly. It may take several tries before we find a balance that feels right for us.

During the first few years of attending my sangha, I barely gave anything monetarily. Not because I couldn't give a couple of bucks, but because I was testing to see if they were really serious about this "freely giving" thing. My Inner Critic had a lot to say to me as well. It let me know that I was unethical, a thief, a bum: *How can you take without compensating their service?* Over time, my suspicions of the sangha diminished. No one reprimanded me for being a freeloader. I didn't get kicked out. I began to relax in my receiving. My inner accusations began to relax as well.

Years later, prompted by discussions of dana within my sangha, I did an inventory of my giving. I realized that I was giving regular monthly donations to four organizations that I loved—and that I was saving no money for myself. Not setting aside a single penny. Once again, I was shocked to see that I was in a position of making myself the Giver while refusing to receive. Setting money aside for my security and peace of mind felt selfish and corrupt when there were so many people in this world who had almost nothing. But now this view was being questioned.

I began noticing the strain that was put on families when their elders encountered health problems. Those who had a lifetime's worth of savings and investments spared their families the stress of a huge financial burden. Having a financial buffer allows many people to attend to unexpected medical bills without going into debt. That financial padding also makes it possible for a person to take much-needed vacations and retreats to recharge, rest, and experience the healing to be found in play. Eliminating one's financial stress frees a person to show up in a more present way and attend to others more effectively, as well as reducing stress-induced health problems. (I could go on, because there are so many practical reasons to set aside money for oneself.) I finally decided to give it a try. For the first time in my life, at age thirty-three, I opened a savings account for myself and set up automatic monthly deposits. In the very next moment, I set up recurring monthly payments to my sangha. It wasn't out of obligation. It came from a place of pure gratitude for what I had been given.

How is it that we come to value giving over receiving? I'm sure not everyone has as rough a go at it as I have, and yet it seems a commonly held view in our society. Pride, fear, and a false sense of individualism drive this belief. When we take a moment to look closer, we notice that everything in this world—in this universe—is in a perpetual state of receiving. Plants cannot exist without the complex systems of weather that bring sunshine, rain, and optimal temperatures to sustain life. Animals cannot exist without plants. And, of course, humans could not exist without the sustenance of plants. With each breath, we receive their oxygen into our bodies, and their nutrients into our bellies with each meal. Our very lives are dependent upon each drop of rain. Martin Luther King Jr. put it so eloquently:

> [A]ll mankind is tied together; all life is interrelated, and we are all caught in an inescapable network of mutuality, tied in a single garment of destiny. Whatever affects one directly, affects all indirectly. For some strange reason I can never be what I ought to be until you are what you ought to be. And you can never be what you ought to be until I am what I ought to be—this is the interrelated structure of reality.[10]

This interdependent web of mutuality requires both giving *and* receiving. One is not more worthy or sacred than the other. In fully receiving a birthday present, a shoulder to cry on, spiritual teachings, or the gift of sexual pleasure, we allow the other person the joy of giving freely, with no strings attached.

None of these is a favor that must be repaid. If it were, it would not be a gift; it would be a transactional exchange. In many cases, expecting a certain favor in response is an act of manipulation.

Throughout my lifetime, I have observed the strings attached to my giving. I have given gifts to earn the other's love in return. I have offered my knowledge in hopes that I would be publicly recognized as wise and valuable. I have given to charity to appease my Inner Critic and prove that I am a good person worthy of love. I have offered sexual favors in desperate attempts to get my partner to never leave me. All of these have left the bitter aftertaste of resentment and shame in my heart. The missing ingredient in all these transactions was *self*-love—and self-love requires a willingness to receive pleasure, to believe in the marrow of my bones that I am worthy of taking in the beauty and joy inherent in this life.

In that moment on the toilet, still trippin' balls in Wisconsin, the sacred vagina in my chest made perfect sense. My heart had been cracked open to the possibility of fully and freely receiving the wondrous gifts of living. The cycle of dana was complete, if only for that moment. I don't suspect the mushroom trip completely cured me of my wrong views and my attachment to being a Giver, but it did peel back my defenses and delusions just long enough for me to glimpse the next path on my spiritual journey. It pointed to the Way and allowed me to see possibilities I had not previously imagined.

However, just as I'd intuited, it did miraculously cure me of my lifelong struggle with vaginismus. When the high was wearing off and my feet were landing back on the ground of normal perception, I made myself a gorgeous bowl of soup from a can, happy to receive the nourishment of the lentils and vegetables. Another mantra popped into my head then: "Whatever you have to give, I'll take it."

Having gone on this wild ride of devils, universal orgasms, and sacred vaginas, taking what was given no longer felt the least bit selfish. Later that evening, I decided to test the effectiveness of the mushroom medicine. I stared at my dilators. Like Jesus's disciple "Doubting" Thomas, I needed proof. I reached for the large one, lubed it up, and slid it in. Easy peasy, lemon squeezy. No contraction, no burning, no pain. It was just as two of my new mantras had told me: "When I think I am open, I am open. Whatever is within me to receive, I receive it."

Just like that, I shut the cover on that chapter of my life. I am now no longer the victim of religious sexual shame. I am a survivor. And I'm ready to thrive.

During my senior year of college, one of my friends gave me a black wooden ring that she had brought back from a study abroad in Brazil. Handing it to me, she said, "This particular type of ring has a certain tradition around it. It represents a particular struggle that the wearer is going through. So you should pick something from your life that you are constantly struggling with, and this ring can be a reminder to you that you are working on healing this struggle." A few years later, when I discovered the diagnosis of my vaginismus, I decided that was what the ring would represent for me. I wore this ring on the ring finger of my right hand for twelve years. And I loved it. Not only did it remind me I was working on this area of myself, but I also allowed it to be a reminder to be gentle and understanding of myself throughout this struggle.

In some subconscious way, I was attached to my vaginismus. It had become such a focal point of my identity. Ironically, as painful and shameful as having vaginismus was, it had also been protective for me. I consider myself fairly sexually charged. I always have been. With my habit of dating addicts and having few boundaries and little self-esteem in my twenties, I could have gotten myself in a whole lot more trouble had it not been for my body's chosen way of self-protection. Now that I am more discerning with the people I date (and now that I'm even beginning to be attracted to healthy people!), I no longer need my pelvic floor to keep assholes—I mean, dicks—out. My impulsive and reckless dating life is over. Finally, my body trusts me to make good choices.

When I got home from the cabin in the Wisconsin woods the day after my mushroom trip, the wooden ring on my finger broke into three pieces. I didn't even hit it on anything. It just broke and fell off. The very next day, I went to a clothing swap with a group of female friends. My dear friend Lynn was getting rid of a ring that looked like either an angel wing or an unfolding lotus flower. I tried it on, and it fit perfectly on the finger where the wooden ring had flung itself away from me the day before. As my spiritual director Janet likes to say with a knowing smile, "This just reeks of God."

A Note about Using Psychedelics

In sharing my story, I am in no way recommending the use of psychedelics or suggesting they are a guaranteed cure to one's physical, emotional, mental, or spiritual struggles. They are not for everyone and should be approached with appropriate caution. Also, note that in most places in the United States, psychedelics are still illegal, even though many cities and states are moving away from criminalizing plant-based medicines, including psilocybin. The use of psychedelics is currently reemerging in scientific and academic studies and is being used in clinical trials in a new field called psychedelic-assisted therapy. With the help of trained psychologists and spiritual leaders, psychedelics are being used in controlled settings to treat PTSD, depression, anxiety, addiction, and even dementia. The results are overwhelmingly successful and positive when used properly, with professional guidance on how to prepare beforehand and how to integrate the experience afterward. Nature-based psychedelics have been used in Indigenous rituals for spiritual healing, growth, and mind/body/emotional integration for as long as humans have been human, usually with the guidance of a traditional healer (aka shaman).

Set and *setting* are two terms that are of key importance when considering the use of psychedelic medicines. Professional healers and therapists recommend an extensive period of mental preparation before engaging in a psychedelic "trip." This includes a regular practice of meditation and awareness of the many layers of the "mind," entering with a clear intention of chosen mindset to guide one's own experience and preparing a safe, sacred space to create a setting that induces comfort, relaxation, and beauty and where the only people present are those you completely love and trust. Without a regular meditation practice, one may get caught in a negative or paranoid mental-looping pattern during a psychedelic trip and be incapable of redirecting oneself away from this negative experience. Other benefits and risks are possible and can be found by searching for the many available resources on psychedelic or entheogenic healing and therapy through podcasts, books, and websites. A good place to start is the book *Your Psilocybin Mushroom Companion* by Michelle Janikian.

Again, my intention is not to advocate for psychedelic use for anyone, but only to share my experience and to explain and resolve my struggles and healing from vaginismus, sexual shame, and religious trauma. You are free to take what you like and leave the rest. This has been a long journey, and my Inner Critic has been involved every step of the way. In hindsight, I can see that so have my Inner Angels and Advocates. While the Inner Critic voices were often distracting because they were so loud, underneath their racket there has been a quiet, steady intuition that it doesn't have to be like this. Something caring and gentle within me had been encouraging me to get help, to change, and to heal all along. By the grace of Godde and the encouragement of many teachers, mentors, and friends, I am learning to listen to that still, small voice of kindness. You also have this voice within you, and you can begin to trust it and listen.

Why Is Receiving So Hard?

For many people, receiving is very difficult, whether that is receiving the love and admiration of a friend or partner, using vacation time to be away from work, or simply accepting a compliment without brushing it off or minimizing it. There are two issues at play here: Pride, and a sense of Unworthiness. At first glance, these may seem to be opposites, but they complement each other with startling consistency.

On the surface, we can see and experience Pride at work. It says things like, *No, thank you. I'm fine. I don't need help.* Or, *I've got this, I'm self-sufficient. But what do you need?* Or, *Oh, this old dress? I got it for two dollars at a garage sale!*

In these moments, there is a sense of being puffed up, a deflecting of assistance and love. Most often, this is a defensive move. If I can tell myself I don't need anyone's help, I can keep my heart safe from rejection. Because *what if* I ask for help, a hug, or a listening ear, and I get turned down? No thanks. Too risky. That would trigger the sense of unworthiness and shame that is waiting just beneath the surface. So why not accept help when it is freely offered? That can also trigger the feeling of unworthiness, of being "less than." When someone gives me something, even when it's out of pure kindness and generosity, it can feel like they are now superior to me. The Giver seems to be higher up on the proverbial ladder than me, the Receiver, who has now been knocked down a few rungs by accepting help. To put myself in this position feels like giving up my power. It feels like I am losing control of my life.

The key phrase in those last sentences is "feels like." It is an illusion, a mental construct. There is no hierarchy between the Giver and the Receiver. The ladder doesn't exist. There is only a circle of equality between all beings. Accepting this requires a sense of true Humility, which is the opposite of Pride. Humility is not humiliation. It is a willingness to see oneself as part of the human race, part of the balance and flow of giving and receiving. This is a huge step, and the Unworthiness is a shadow that must be faced and befriended, like all the other Inner Critics. If we do not explore it, it will keep running the show, hiding behind the mask of Pride.

So how to move from Unworthiness and Pride into a sense of Humility? This cannot be done without training ourselves in Gratitude. A thankful heart is wide awake and paying attention to all the ways that life is supporting us *already*. We are already receiving innumerable gifts each day: oxygen, clean water, and a functioning body. What follows are a couple of exercises to warm you up to the practice of receiving support and love. Without a willingness to receive, we won't get very far on the spiritual path. And we certainly won't move beyond the entrapments of our Inner Critic. We must truly believe we deserve better and open our minds and hearts to experience provision, contentment, and joy.

YOUR TURN!
Inner Work Exercises

1. Awaken to Gratitude

Choose one activity you do every day. Once you've chosen it, picture yourself doing each step of this activity in your mind's eye. Where are you? What are you wearing? What material items are needed for this activity? What mental faculties or physical abilities do you need to do this activity? Notice how many things need to be in place for this moment to become possible. Who or what was involved in the process of bringing you to this moment?

I'll give you an example: My activity is watching a movie while sitting on my couch. To do this simple activity, I need the following:

- Functioning eyesight and hearing.

- A safe and warm house in which to watch movies.

- A computer that was designed, assembled, and shipped by many people who gave their creativity and intellect to a cause greater than themselves.

- My functioning brain, which can process the incoming information at a lightning-fast pace and which I received through both biological processes and the mysterious gift of consciousness.

- A couch that is made of many different materials, including wood, cotton, metal, and polyester, all of which started as elements given from the earth and then harvested and processed by humans who gave their time and talents to make the couch a reality.

- The popcorn I'm eating, which began as a seed that received water, sunshine, nutrients from the soil, farmers who tended to the plant and harvested the corn, many machines, factory workers who processed the kernels and packaged them, accountants, CEOs, truck drivers, grocery store workers . . . and on and on.

Since the answers to this question are almost infinite, set a timer for five minutes and see how many things you can write down (or name to a friend out loud). When the timer goes off, stop, breathe deeply, and place one hand on your heart. Read each item listed and say, "Thank you." Notice the impact this has on your inner stories of individualism and autonomy. You are already immensely supported by the whole Universe, and you've been receiving Her gifts all along! Allow a few minutes to savor this reality, simply breathing and noticing any feelings or thoughts that come up. Receive them all with love. Then, slowly, repeat these affirmations out loud to yourself:

> I notice and am grateful for the many gifts I receive each moment.
>
> I am loved and supported by the whole Universe.
>
> I am not alone on this journey.
>
> Help is available and abundant.
>
> I can ask for help and support when I need it.
>
> I easily ask for help and support.
>
> I receive love and support with humility and ease.
>
> It feels wonderful to be a human being who is equal to all others.
>
> When it is my turn to give, I do so with generosity and goodwill.
>
> Thank you. Thank you. Thank you.

2. Inventory Your Inner Critic Characters

Revisit each of the Inner Critic characters you have discovered in yourself as you read this book. Notice if any of them speak to you about your unworthiness in any way. Write down their names and briefly jot down their messages of unworthiness, unlovableness, or self-doubt. While you are feeling confident about the abundance of love and support in the Universe, gently inform your Inner Critics that you have good news for them. Then, inform them of your new Truths by telling them the affirmations listed in the first exercise above. If they protest in any way or criticize you for being naive, gently but firmly tell them, "This is not a debate. You can have your opinions, but this is what I know to be true, and I'm sticking to it." Then return to your feelings of gratitude.

By now, if you have been doing the exercises throughout this book, you have developed enough awareness to know that believing the lies of the Inner Critic is a choice. Choose differently. Listen instead to the still, quiet voice that lives both within and all around you. The one that says, "You are loved and supported. It is safe to love yourself. It is safe to receive Love."

CHAPTER 16:
Detaching from the Inner Critic

Where and when God finds you ready, God must act and overflow into you, just as when the air is clear and pure, the sun must overflow into it and cannot refrain from doing that.
—Meister Eckhart

Now it is time. Time to let go of all that holds us back, harms us, and harms others. Time to release everything that is not serving to support the flowering of our greatest good, our healing, and the emergence of our Essence, our Highest Self. The world needs us to be the best version of ourselves.

While this all sounds fantastic, often fear or doubt will arise at the thought of change—even positive change. This is normal. Our Inner Critics have been longtime companions of ours. While they haven't been very kind, they have become like friends: familiar, predictable, and (in some ways) comforting. It can feel ludicrous to give them up. (*Aren't they what make me . . . well, me? Don't they define my personality? They protect me from pain! What would I be without them?*)

The sixth step in the Twelve Step program reads, "We were entirely ready to have God remove all these defects of character." Entirely ready? *Really?* How does one become entirely ready? And how do we know when we're ready enough to move on to step seven, which states, "We humbly asked God to remove our shortcomings"? (As always, feel free to translate *God* to a word or name you like.)

While working on step six for the first time, I found myself deep in meditation, and an image arose. I could see all of my patterns of criticism, self-doubt, self-righteousness, fear, and anger in their many forms wrapped around my heart, constricting it. Previously, it had felt like they were holding me securely, like a seatbelt. But in this moment, I could see they were stunting my growth and limiting my options. As if it were tangled yarn wound tightly in a ball, I slowly began to pull it apart, piece by piece, to examine it. As I pulled the metaphorical string out of my chest, it piled up in a heap in front of me. It just kept coming. I kept pulling. There were all my defects, my unskillful patterns, my manipulative ego tricks, laid bare for the world to see—and I was presented with a choice. Once I had seen it, I could not unsee it. But I *could* choose to walk around dragging this ball of string behind me, letting it weigh me down, just in case I needed some of it again. Or I could cut the cord. But I was afraid of the emptiness that I'd find within me if these old companions were released. Conflicted, and wanting to tend honestly to this pain, this song poured out from me:

Scan the code with your phone's camera to watch Chelsea sing the song on YouTube

"Pile of String"

I am pulling, pulling, pulling out the heartstrings,
Strings of shame and fear that kept me tied,
Wrapped so tight around this fragile heart of mine,
So much string I almost died.

There's a pile of string on my floor, and it's ten feet high.
When pain is pleasure, you know you're doing life all wrong.
I could cut the cord and say goodbye,
But am I finally ready to move on?

DETACHING FROM THE INNER CRITIC

Into Love, into Light, into Peace, into Wholeness,
Who would I be without this shame?
I'd be empty, with room to fill it with a Mystery.
Is it time to change my name?
To Love, Forgiveness, Love?
I could be Love, Forgiveness, Love.

I was never told I had a choice,
To stop listening to those thoughts running through my head.
Thoughts are just thoughts, they're not God's voice.
So now I choose to listen to my heart instead.

Now as fears run by, I don't chase them anymore.
There's a freedom and relief in letting go.
But I still find bits of string on the kitchen floor.
Just sweep them up and let them know . . .

That now you're Love, you're Light, you're Peace, you are Wholeness.
Can't believe you held on so long to your pain.
Now you're empty, with room to fill it with a Mystery,
And it's time to change your name
To Love, Freedom, Love.
Love, Freedom, Love.

Did you think that you could define me?
Did you think that box was for me?
Did you think that Godde was tiny?
Did you think that hate would set you free?

We choose Love and Light; we choose Peace and Wholeness.
It feels so good to let go of this shame.
Now we're empty, with room to fill it with the Great Mystery.
It's past time we changed our name

To Love, Forgiveness, Love.

Love and Freedom . . . Love, Forgiveness, Love.

The amazing surprise I rediscovered here is that a Power greater than ourselves is what transforms us. Yes, there is work for us to do. Yes, we need to be diligent in being honest with ourselves, surrounding ourselves with loving friends and mentors, attending to our pain, and developing a daily spiritual practice. But most of the "work" is about *letting go.*

Look again at the wording of steps six and seven of the Twelve Step program. The key is that it is Godde who removes the defects and shortcomings, not us. If we could have done it ourselves, we would have done it by now! Don't let the term *Godde* trip you up if you're not into theism. It is just pointing to something greater than our ego. I've discovered through my inner work that the Universe has our greatest good in its plan and will remove our defects. The Buddha, Dhamma, and Sangha are a tried-and-true refuge that purify practitioners' minds and hearts. Mother Nature, Spirit, the Intelligent Energy that animates all life, Consciousness Itself, the Tao, the Way, our Inner Wisdom, or our True Essence are all equally appropriate replacements for the metaphorical term *Godde*. After all, they are all pointing to the Great Mystery that cannot be named: the "I Am that I Am."

If this all sounds like foolishness to you, that's okay. Find a word that works best for you, and try it out. Call it Puppies and Unicorns, if you'd like. What can it hurt? Without something or someone to turn your struggles over to, you're left with only options like this:

- "If I just try harder, I can fix myself. Buckle down!"
- "I've got to hurry up and figure this out!"
- "I must be doing something wrong, because I'm still falling into the same old patterns."
- "I've tried everything to change myself. Maybe it's better to just give up."

Notice how your body reacts when you allow yourself to feel into the above strategies and views. Does your body tighten or loosen? Does your mind quiet down or speed up? Does your heart expand or contract? Are these views comforting or stressful?

Also, pay attention to how your body, heart, and mind respond to the following choices. Insert your favorite word for your Higher Power in each blank space:

- "I let go of the need to cure, improve, or fix myself. I turn my healing process over to _____."
- "I trust that _____ will remove my Inner Critics and my shortcomings when _____ is ready and when I am ready."
- "My only job is to let go, trust, listen, and be willing."
- "Without my Inner Critic babbling away, there will be room for the voices of Wisdom and Love to naturally emerge."
- "I am ready to turn my shortcomings and my Inner Critic voices over to _____."
- "_____, this committee of Inner Critics is now yours. I turn them over to you."
- "May _____ lead me into deeper joy, peace, love, and happiness. I trust _____."
- "I trust the natural process of my mental, emotional, and spiritual evolution."

Take some time to write down and say these phrases out loud to yourself each day. Feel free to add your own phrases. Then sit with them and breathe. Breathe in trust, breathe out stress.

As we embark upon this deeper level of spiritual exploration and surrender, it is important to tread tenderly. A gentle approach is needed. When I began writing this book, I asked my spiritual director to give me feedback about areas in which I've been especially critical. She reminded me that "this self-analysis business is not a witch hunt!" We needn't obsess about finding and focusing on our flaws. Burning ourselves at the stake for being human is not the goal here.

Instead, we can place our attention on our Inner Angels, our Inner Advocates, our Inner Wisdom. (These are names I use interchangeably.) If the Inner Critic serves to keep us trapped inside the familiar and limited box of our ego personality, Inner Angels are the voices that coax us out into freedom. They want us to grow, explore, have fun, and evolve. They are that little nudge inside that says, "This is possible!" and they dare us to take healthy risks for our benefit and the benefit of all beings. So often, I have ignored the whisper that says, "Do it! You are capable! It won't kill you!" When my gnome Sharpakyrie jumps in with a pep talk, I frequently shun his optimism as recklessness. Logic and skepticism arise to wrestle his foolishness back underground. But thankfully, he persists. Light is difficult to fully extinguish; and eventually, the soul gives in to its deepest longing for freedom.

In the Bible, every time an angel shows up with a message (because their main job is to deliver messages), they always start by saying, "Do not be afraid." How peculiar, that humans are predictably petrified by Good News. We shrink away from our angel's messages, afraid the Light will undo us and put us in harm's way. Just so, our Inner Angels have come to expect that we will fear and dismiss them. So they are persistent, showing up again and again, speaking through dreams, daydreams, and our heart's deepest desires. At some point, through our willingness to wrestle with them, we finally listen. As frequently quoted as this is, our souls and psyches can always benefit from hearing this passage from Marianne Williamson one more time:

> Our deepest fear is not that we are inadequate. Our deepest fear is that we are powerful beyond measure. It is our light, not our darkness, that most frightens us. We ask ourselves: Who am I to be brilliant, gorgeous, talented, fabulous? Actually, who are you *not* to be? You are a child of God. Your playing small does not serve the world. There is nothing enlightened about shrinking so that other people won't feel insecure around you. We are all meant to shine, as children do. We were born to make manifest the glory of God that is within us. It's not just in some of us; it's in everyone. And as we let our own light shine, we unconsciously give other people permission to do the same. As we are liberated from our own fear, our presence automatically liberates others.[11]

There is nothing selfish about self-love. There is no arrogance in self-confidence. These are the greatest gifts we can give the world.

DETACHING FROM THE INNER CRITIC

The Enneagram's Lost Childhood Messages

While there are many wonderful and fascinating parts of the Enneagram, the one that I find most related to awakening our Inner Advocate is the teaching around the Lost Childhood Message. It states that each of us, as children, began to interpret a fundamental flaw about ourselves at some very early age. There was a certain message about our true nature that our mind, heart, and/or soul needed to integrate, but this message got lost. As innocence faded, fear set in, and we began basing all our behavior around our particular imagined deficit. The messages are called "lost" because we *had* them at some point.

For example, an Enneagram One's Lost Childhood Message is "You are good." When this message gets lost, Ones internalize the opposite belief of "I am bad, corrupt, and/or evil." As babies and young children, of course Ones were pure and good. But Ones as children typically feel criticized and not good enough, like they're punished for mistakes or for expressing emotion. So the ego develops a fixation around judging between right and wrong, good and bad, because they are trying so hard to avoid mistakes and maintain self-control. Since they have lost touch with their inherent *birthright* of Goodness, they are always (subconsciously) anxious about doing something wrong that would define them as corrupt, bad, or evil. For Ones to begin their path back toward wholeness and healing, they need to reclaim the truth of "I am good."

Every one of these messages is a message for *all* of us, but one of them in particular is at the core of our ego's motivations and fixations. This piece of the Enneagram can shine much-needed light on our type and on the direction of our growth path. Notice that the subsequent "interpretations" are the foundation and structure of the ego personality's prison. These messages are not a result of specific styles of parenting. They are the way in which the child has misinterpreted their experience. No child had parents who could perfectly mirror back and affirm their beautiful Essence qualities, so the child had to bury a part of themselves to try to fit into a world filled with ego-driven adults. If a child has had a high level of abuse or neglect, their connection to their innate goodness and lovability weakens. For these children, the ego has had to solidify even more to protect them, and the Lost Childhood Message is much more difficult to believe (though not impossible to uncover with the help of good therapy and other support).

Here are the Lost Childhood Messages for each Enneagram type:

1. Enneagram Ones: "I am good." Interpreted as, "I am in danger of being evil, corrupt, or bad. I need to stay on the straight and narrow to avoid the slippery slope! My moral superiority and integrity prove my goodness."

2. Enneagram Twos: "I am lovable." Interpreted as, "No one will love me unless I'm helping others, unless I'm needed. I've gotta give more to prove and earn my lovableness!"

3. Enneagram Threes: "I am valuable." Interpreted as, "I am only valuable when I'm accomplishing great things! Proving my value through my impressive capabilities will bring me the love and attention I desire."

4. Enneagram Fours: "I belong." Interpreted as, "I'm a misfit. I am different from everyone else, and no one understands me. I will prove that I belong by making myself noticeably special to draw love toward me and by withdrawing into my inner world of feelings and fantasy."

5. Enneagram Fives: "I am enough." Interpreted as, "I am not enough to gain love and security on my own, so I'll spend my energy gathering knowledge, skills, and ideas, and detaching from others and from my feelings. This proves my competence, my enoughness."

6. Enneagram Sixes: "I am safe." Interpreted as, "I am in danger. Life and people are unpredictable. My defense against harm is doubting and questioning—even doubting my instincts and Inner Guidance. By preparing for the worst, I will prove I'm safe."

7. Enneagram Sevens: "I am free." Interpreted as, "I could be trapped! Best to avoid this by staying on the move, focusing on all my positive options, and creating pleasurable experiences! Keeping the 'fun pedal' to the metal proves that I am free!"

8. Enneagram Eights: "I can be vulnerable." Interpreted as, "I mustn't show weakness—only Power! Emotions and tenderness are vulnerability, and that will get me hurt. I'll make myself as big as possible to protect myself (and others). My strength, productivity, energy, and fast pace prove my Power."

9. Enneagram Nines: "I matter." Interpreted as, "My presence doesn't matter. My feelings and needs are unimportant, so I'll keep a low profile and merge with others. I cannot affect change. Making others feel comfortable and keeping the peace proves that I matter."

Each of these Lost Childhood Messages is incredibly heartbreaking—and incredibly ironic. How could Nines believe they don't matter? We all love them in their natural gifts of sweetness, inclusion, and peacekeeping; and when they are absent, we miss them fiercely. Likewise, how could Threes be worried about proving their capability when the rest of us could never keep up with their work ethic, confidence, and enthusiasm? Why would Eights hide their tender side when their big hearts are what make them so darn lovable? They don't need to prove they are powerful, because even when sitting in silence, we would still feel the strength emanating from an Eight!

Taking the time to feel the grief of our Lost Childhood Message is part of the path to reclaiming it. We are all striving for something we believe is lost about ourselves, but it turns out we have just lost *sight* of it! It never went anywhere! It was there, waiting for us all along, under layers of stories, delusions, fears, greed, and anger—in other words, beneath the much louder voice of our Inner Critic. We have been searching for it in all the wrong places, with all the wrong methods. The answer is not outside ourselves, and it will never be found through the striving of the ego. It is *within* us, and the only way to access what we've been seeking is through Presence. Presence is the moment-to-moment loving awareness of what is happening within us in our body, heart, and mind. Presence is a spacious, healing, and ineffable balm. We know we are Present when we are accepting all things *just as they are.*

If only we could see ourselves the way our true friends see us, the way our pets see us, the way the Divine sees us! We *are* seen as good, as lovable, as capable, as belonging, as enough, as safe, as free, as having permission to be vulnerable, as someone who matters—*so much.* Not only are we seen as each of these things, but we are also each of these things because they are our birthright.

Here's the real kicker: When we begin to believe our Lost Childhood Message, to truly accept it as truth in our bones, *this removes the need for an Inner*

Critic. Think about it. This lost message is the missing piece of the puzzle. It is the message your Inner Angels have been trying to get through to you all along! With no anxiety around trying to *prove* and *perform* our goodness, our lovableness, our value, our freedom, etc., the rigid boundaries of the ego dissolve. We are suddenly free to make mistakes, to fail, to honor our feelings, to relax, to let go, *and to trust that none of this has any bearing on our self-worth or true happiness.*

As an Enneagram One who has been striving for perfection her whole life, I became extremely averse to making mistakes, and the slightest slipup would send my Inner Critic into a full-blown rage. It wouldn't take much. If I clumsily dropped my pencil on the floor, didn't know the definition of a big word someone just used, or woke up five minutes later than I had planned, it would send my Inner Critic into an uproar. Seriously. Dropping my pencil or not knowing how to spell a word would ruin my whole day.

I began to notice major shifts after working for a while with internalizing my Lost Childhood Message. Even though I didn't believe it at first, just naming the possibility that "I am good" despite my flaws brought me a sense of relief. I began using "I am good" as a mantra. I even wrote it into a catchy ditty to the tune of "Three Blind Mice" so that I purposefully couldn't get it out of my head:

> I am good, I am good!
>
> Godde sees good, Godde sees good!
>
> Godde made it all, and it all is good,
>
> From the country ranch to the city hood.
>
> That means I'm good. I am good!

Over time, things began shifting. One time when I spilled something, I simply said, "Oops," and went on with my day without a moment of self-flagellation. It was shocking (in a good way). When I made a horrible mistake at work and was called into my boss's office to be reprimanded, I kept my cool, admitted my wrongs, and stated what I would do differently next time. I then walked away without a shred of self-loathing. It was a miracle! My deepest wound that I thought would never leave me was healing. But that was only because I asked Presence to come with me into that office.

The same freedom is possible for all of us, regardless of our particular childhood or adulthood wounds. None of us is destined to live in pain or to perpetually reenact our trauma. Change is possible. Change is inevitable. In this amazing era of globalized resources, spiritual and psychological healing methods from all over the world are at our fingertips. We have exactly what we need to enter the next stage of our transformation and maturation, both individually and collectively. This book and the exercises within are just a start, but I promise they are a very good start. Over time, through the eyes of patience and compassion, our healing will unfold. Like a many-petaled lotus flower atop the water, it is already unfolding.

YOUR TURN!
Inner Work Exercises

1. Contact Your Positive Childhood Voice

We've all had positive moments of happiness and freedom in our childhood, even if we come from difficult family backgrounds. The following visualization is one way to reconnect with the positive, encouraging, self-confident, creative, silly, peaceful, or loving voice within you with which you may have lost touch. You may want to record yourself reading this slowly so that you can use it as a guided meditation:

Close your eyes. Take a moment to think back to your earliest happy memory. What were you doing? What were you feeling? What kinds of things were you saying aloud or to yourself? Allow yourself to really reconnect with this memory, recalling colors, sounds, smells, tactile textures, or tastes. This happy child is still a part of you, within you somewhere.

Now, imagine yourself sitting down with this child in a safe place. Take a good look at each other. Smile. Then ask the child, "What would you like to tell me?" Without forcing an answer, just listen within. Allow the child to speak, be silly, throw a tantrum, or cry. What message does this child have for you today?

Continue to breathe and listen. When you have connected with a message, word, or feeling from your Inner Child, thank them, tell them you look forward to spending time with them again soon, and then open your eyes.

2. Use Your Lost Childhood Message as a Mantra

Not sure of your Enneagram type? No problem. Just choose one Lost Childhood Message from the earlier list that feels like it is calling to you. It's probably the one that feels most uncomfortable to fully trust. (You can't hurt yourself by choosing the "wrong" one, as they are all medicinal. You can eventually use them all!) Once you have chosen your Message, here are some ways of working with it:

- Sit in a comfortable position and repeat it silently in your mind while breathing deeply. Imagine breathing this mantra into every nook and cranny of your body, filling yourself up with this truth, leaving no part of yourself untouched by it. As the Inner Critic comes up, just tell it with disinterest, "Thanks for your opinion, but not now," and go back to your mantra.

- Do the above mantra meditation while walking, while washing dishes, or every time you go up or down a staircase.

- Write your Message into a meaningful song, a catchy ditty, a piece of artwork, or a poem.

- Look at yourself in the mirror and repeat your Message out loud to yourself. Smile, and take in this good news. Get silly with it. Cry with it. Feel the numbing walls you have constructed against it. Whatever happens is okay.

Final Blessing

*There are a thousand ways to kneel and kiss the ground.
There are a thousand ways to go home again.*
—Rumi

Congratulations! You've made it to the end! By now, you know how to name, tame, and transform your Inner Critic; and you'll have these tools with you on your lifelong journey. In a nutshell, here's the process:

1. Name It: As long as we don't see the Inner Critic clearly, nothing will change. Take a deeper look. Get to know the shadowy parts of yourself, the stories they are telling you, and their motivations.

2. Tame It: The taming of an Inner Critic is like taming a wolf. You would not try to beat it into submission because you know it would maul you as soon as you turn your back. Between your bare hands and the wolf's teeth and claws, the wolf will surely win in a fight. The way to tame a wolf is to treat it with kindness, generosity, gentleness, and extreme patience. Eventually, you'll get close to it, no longer afraid to be near it as if it is a wild beast.

3. Transform It: The way out of the pain is through compassion and curiosity. Only Love will change the Inner Critic into an Inner Advocate. The last mystery ingredient in this recipe is Surrender. We must let go of trying to control our process and instead allow it to unfold, trusting that we are cared for and carried.

It is my sincere wish that something I have said has been of use to you, dear reader. You are welcome and encouraged to take what you liked and leave the rest. As suggested by the above quote from Rumi, not all of my suggestions will fit you. Your life journey has been different from mine, and your Inner Critic's messages are unique to you. Your wounds are different and will therefore require different medicine. However, the themes of presence, compassion, self-awareness, and community presented in this book are universal to the Homecoming process. Therefore, regardless of which spiritual practices you choose to adopt, my prayer for you is the same. Let these words soak into all the deepest parts of you, and repeat them for yourself:

> May you find abiding happiness and peace.
>
> May you be free from the suffering of inner torment and criticism.
>
> May you befriend your Inner Critic so that the internal war may cease.
>
> May you fully forgive yourself for your humanity, and others for theirs.
>
> May you be gentle with yourself always, in all ways.
>
> May you find humor and beauty in your flaws.
>
> May you feel gratitude and awe for the opportunity to wake up in this lifetime.
>
> May Presence, Wisdom, and Love light your way home.
>
> Amen. May it be so.

References

1. The Christian Godde Project, Shawna R. B. Atteberry, and Mark M. Mattison, *The Divine Feminine Version of the New Testament*, 2nd ed. (self-pub, CreateSpace, 2017).

2. Barbara McAfee, "Brain Rats by Barbara McAfee," posted May 7, 2019, YouTube video, 03:14, https://www.youtube.com/watch?v=ZOuzuMx9wP4.

3. Lama Tsultrim Allione, "How to Feed Your Demons," *Lion's Roar*, May 19, 2022, https://www.lionsroar.com/how-to-practice-feeding-your-demons/.

4. IFS Institute (home page), accessed October 2018, https://ifs-institute.com/.

5. Eckhart Tolle, *A New Earth: Awakening to Your Life's Purpose* (New York: Plume, 2005), 30–33.

6. Brené Brown, *Daring Greatly: How the Courage to Be Vulnerable Transforms the Way We Live, Love, Parent, and Lead* (New York: Avery Publishing Group, 2015), 89 and 92.

7. Louise Hay, *You Can Heal Your Life* (Carlsbad, California: Hay House, 1999), 180.

8. Hay, *You Can Heal Your Life*, 180.

9. Martin Luther King Jr., "Remaining Awake Through a Great Revolution," transcript of commencement address at Oberlin College, June 1965, https://www2.oberlin.edu/external/EOG/BlackHistoryMonth/MLK/CommAddress.html.

10. Marianne Williamson, *A Return to Love: Reflections on the Principles of "A Course in Miracles"* (New York: Harper Collins, 1992), 165.

Suggested Reading to Take You Deeper

The Enneagram
- *The Complete Enneagram: 27 Paths to Greater Self-Knowledge* by Beatrice Chestnut, PhD
- *The Enneagram: Understanding Yourself and the Others in Your Life* by Helen Palmer
- *The Enneagram of Passions and Virtues: Finding the Way Home* by Sandra Maitri
- *The Wisdom of the Enneagram: The Complete Guide to Psychological and Spiritual Growth for the Nine Personality Types* by Don Richard Riso and Russ Hudson

Buddhist Teachings and Practices
- *Lovingkindness: The Revolutionary Art of Happiness* by Sharon Salzberg
- *Peace Is Every Step: The Path of Mindfulness in Everyday Life* by Thich Nhat Hanh
- *Radical Acceptance: Embracing Your Life with the Heart of a Buddha* by Tara Brach
- *Unhindered: A Mindful Path Through the Five Hindrances* by Gil Fronsdal

Contemplative Christianity
- *Falling Upward: A Spirituality for the Two Halves of Life* by Richard Rohr
- *The Holy Trinity and the Law of Three: Discovering the Radical Truth at the Heart of Christianity* by Cynthia Bourgeault
- *Intimacy with God: An Introduction to Centering Prayer* by Thomas Keating
- *The Universal Christ: How a Forgotten Reality Can Change Everything We See, Hope for, and Believe* by Richard Rohr

About the Author

Chelsea Forbrook is a spiritual director and Enneagram educator based in Minneapolis, Minnesota. She takes great delight in making spiritual principles and practices easy and accessible for all. She teaches a ten-month experiential Enneagram course for personal transformation, is the creator of the Enneaplaque (a meditation tool for awakening), and hosts a podcast called *The Enneagram of Essence*. She is currently the president of Enneagram Minnesota, a chapter of the International Enneagram Association.

When she's not working, Chelsea is zipping around Minneapolis on her bike, gardening, laughing with friends, joining conversations and actions for social justice, reading, writing, painting, and singing songs to her precious dog, Chancho.

To learn more about Chelsea's offerings,
visit chelseaforbrook.com.